Notting Hill Gate
Workbook 5A

für Klasse 9 an Gesamtschulen

Verlag Moritz Diesterweg
Frankfurt am Main

Notting Hill Gate

Workbook 5A
Differenzierende Ausgabe, Advanced Course
für Klasse 9 an Gesamtschulen

Herausgegeben von: Christoph Edelhoff
Erarbeitet von: Otfried Börner, Ingrid Gebhard, Pat Jüngst, Phil Mothershaw-Rogalla, Hannelore Senff und Jürgen Wrobel
sowie Pamela Hanus, Huub Rutten und Frank van Ruyssevelt
Fachliche Beratung: Cordula Dopichei, Rolf-Olaf Geisler, Klaus-Dieter von Kaminietz, Margot Schlömer und Elke Serafin

Weitere Zusatzmaterialien zum Schülerbuch (3-425-10460-8)
- CD zum Schülerbuch (Best.-Nr. 3-425-10465-9)
- Teacher's Manual (Best.-Nr. 3-425-10463-2)

ISBN 3-425-**10461**-6

Bildungshaus Schroedel Diesterweg
Bildungsmedien GmbH & Co. KG
Verlag Moritz Diesterweg
Hedderichstraße 108–110
60596 Frankfurt am Main

Druck A 987 654 321 / Jahr 2007 06 05 04 03

Alle Drucke der Serie A sind im Unterricht parallel verwendbar,
da bis auf die Behebung von Druckfehlern untereinander unverändert.
Die letzte Zahl bezeichnet das Jahr dieses Druckes.

Redaktion: Daniel Shatwell
Illustrationen: Ulf Marckwort, Kassel
Umschlaggestaltung: Boros, Wuppertal
Satz und Repro: Fotosatz Griesheim GmbH, Griesheim
Druck und Verarbeitung: Media-Print Informationstechnologie GmbH, Bad Homburg

Beautiful nature – natural beauty

1

A1 A very personal questionnaire

1. How often do you wash your hair?

- ☐ every day
- ☐ every second day
- ☐ twice a week
- ☐ once a week

2. How often do you take a shower?

- ☐ every day
- ☐ every second day
- ☐ twice a week
- ☐ once a week

3. How many different chemicals[1] are in your shampoo? Have a guess.

- ☐ between 1 and 5
- ☐ between 6 and 12
- ☐ between 13 and 20

4. Do you use any of these?

	regularly	sometimes	never
deodorant	☐	☐	☐
lipstick[2]	☐	☐	☐
make-up	☐	☐	☐
aftershave	☐	☐	☐
hair dye[3]	☐	☐	☐
perfume	☐	☐	☐
body lotion	☐	☐	☐
mascara	☐	☐	☐

5. Do YOU think cosmetics should be tested

	Yes	No
... on animals?	☐	☐
... on people?	☐	☐
... not on animals or people?	☐	☐

6. Animals are very often used in tests. Which of these would YOU use?

	Yes	No
mice	☐	☐
rabbits	☐	☐
chimpanzees	☐	☐
birds	☐	☐
dogs	☐	☐
cats	☐	☐
rats	☐	☐
guinea pigs	☐	☐

7. How many animals are used in tests in German labs[4] every year? Have a guess.

- ☐ about 500,000
- ☐ about 1,000,000
- ☐ about 1,500,000
- ☐ about 2,000,000

[1]chemical = *Chemikalie*; [2]lipstick = *Lippenstift*;
[3]dye = *Farbe*; [4]lab = *Labor*

A2 Talking about testing

Read TB A2 and match up the sentence halves. Write down the complete sentences.

1. Susie thinks it's cruel
2. The "Anti-Experiments on Animals" group said there was no point in
3. Susie doesn't think it is necessary
4. Pete says animal experiments
5. Susie didn't want
6. Pete said that if an experiment is carefully done
7. The hairdresser didn't understand

a. are necessary to develop new drugs and vaccines.
b. what Susie was talking about.
c. and the animals don't suffer, then it's OK.
d. to test cosmetics on animals.
e. to experiment on animals.
f. testing drugs on animals.
g. to hear all of Pete's examples.

A3 Getting ready for a discussion

The following expressions can be used in a discussion. Which list would you put them in?

1 expressing an opinion

2 giving reasons

3 agreeing

4 disagreeing

5 half-agreeing

6 asking for more information

In my view / opinion ...
Don't you think that ...?
Yes, that's very true.
I don't think so.
I feel / believe that ...
Well, it's a fact that ...
That's quite right.
My view / opinion is that ...
Could you say that again, please?
I agree.
That's what I think.
What do you mean by that?
That's what I feel too.
It seems to me that ...
The reason / point is ...
Well, you see ...
I think so too.
I'm not so sure about that.
I'm afraid I can't agree with you there.
Well, possibly, but ...
I beg your pardon?
Yes, I suppose so but ...
Could you explain that, please?
I'm convinced[1] that ...
No, that's just not true.
No, that's absolutely wrong.
I'm afraid you're wrong there.
Well, yes, but ...
Yes, perhaps you're right there.
I think so because ...

[1]convinced = *überzeugt*

A4 Puzzle it out

a) Fill in the correct words and you will find the solution.

1. This is used to stop an illness.
2. They can make you look pretty.
3. This is what you can see on TV.
4. People who do not care about the feelings of others are…
5. This is what you get at the hairdresser's.
6. You can feel this when you break a leg.
7. This is another word for medicine.
8. This is a kind of medicine.
9. You use it to wash your hair.
10. These are done to test something new.

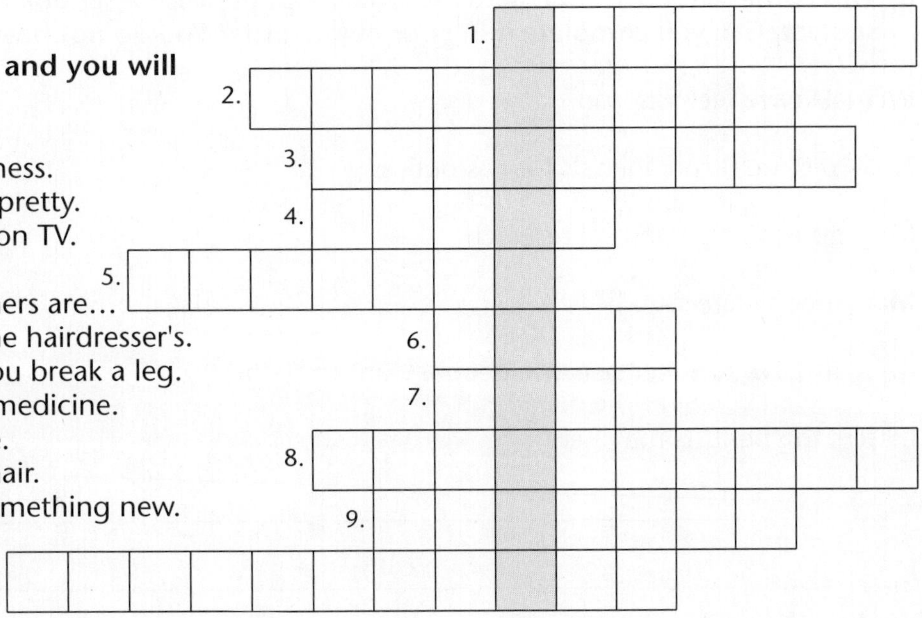

b) Find your own definitions for these words:

rabbit | hairdresser | cat | vegetarian | diary | argument

**c) Use words you know to make your own puzzle.
Give it to a partner. Can he / she understand your definitions?**

A5 Opinions

a) What are they saying? Fill in the balloons.

portfolio

b) This is the first part of an acrostic which a pupil from a school in Hamburg wrote on this subject. Can you complete it in your own words? You do not have to have the same opinion.

Animals have feelings, too.

No experiments on animals for cosmetics.

It is important for medical research.

Many people are saved.

Animals have to suffer because people want to be pretty.

Letters to scientists may help.

T ____

E ____

S ____

T ____

I ____

N ____

G ____

c) Work with a partner. One of you is a scientist who works in a laboratory testing cosmetics on animals, one of you a person against animal testing. You can a) prepare letters to each other, b) interview each other, c) prepare a newspaper article on the basis of the arguments, d) do your own task on this subject.

A6 No point in testing

wbw 25, 26 28, 77

Fill in the ing-nouns or to-infinitives of the following verbs:

buy – colour – declare – lend – play – test – torture – use – wash

1. Some companies gave up________________ animals for their tests.
2. There's really no point in ________________ your hair now – do it after you come back from ________________ football.
3. Every cosmetic company should have ________________ if their product has been tested on animals.
4. Susie doesn't believe that it is necessary ________________ animals in order ________________ cosmetics.

5. People can express their opinion by ______________________ products not tested on animals.

6. Why don't you use my brush for ______________________ your cheeks?

7. I'm quite used to ______________________ my things to others.

A7 Using the word-by-word grammar

a) Look at page 152, window 34. Read it and look for examples in TB A2 and in the rest of the theme.

tip Look at page 129 in your TB for more help with the word-by-word grammar.

b) Make a grammar tree – start with your window like this:

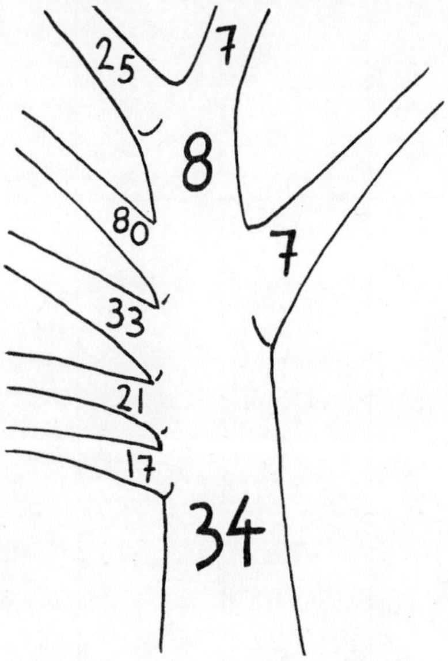

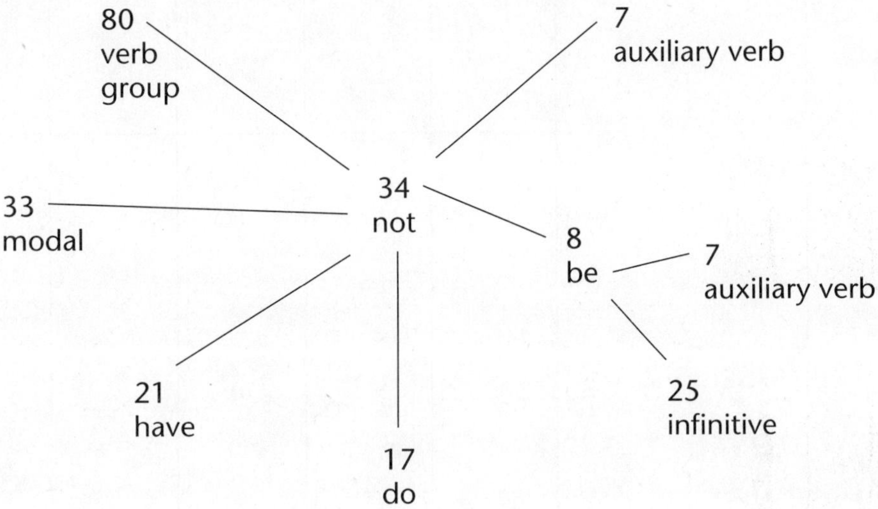

Read the windows. Find examples of different points and make a collage class tree.

c) You can make trees like this for every theme. Add each tree to the collage and you will have a forest of grammar points.

d) Try to explain one or two of the windows in your own words. Look for examples in the texts in theme 1.

e) Read this sentence.
There is an experiment on a mouse in the picture.

Three of the grammar points in this sentence are: *an experiment, on a mouse, in the picture.* Two of the windows for these in the wbw grammar are *a/an* and *prepositions.* Can you find the third?

1

portfolio

B1 A reading record

While you are reading TB B1 or B3 you can fill in the reading record. It can help you understand the text. It is not necessary to write complete sentences – notes will do. Pause after each sentence and check if you want to write anything down.
A reading record is something personal. Your friends or classmates will end up with completely different records. This could be a good start for a discussion about the text.

READING RECORD

Text: ____________________

Date: __________

a good thing?	a bad thing?	interesting	not clear

B2 Living in captivity

a) Read TB B1 again. It can be divided into six paragraphs. Use your reading record to help you find a heading for each paragraph.

1. ______________________________
2. ______________________________
3. ______________________________
4. ______________________________
5. ______________________________
6. ______________________________

b) Now write down in one or two sentences what each of the paragraphs is about.

B3 Kept in tanks

Join these sentence halves for a summary of the text. Is it similar to your sentences for WB B2?

1. The orca is	a. because people want to make money.
2. It does not chase	b. tricks which they would not do in the wild.
3. In the wild,	c. also known as the killer whale.
4. They are caught	d. kept in huge concrete tanks.
5. They are taught	e. about the life of captive orcas.
6. The orcas are	f. orcas stay together in large families.
7. They are often	g. humans but other whales.
8. Free Willy is a film	h. ill because they are kept in captivity.

B4 A matter of time

a) Make lists of phrases which belong to the past, the present and the future.

wbw 76

past	present	future
last week	*now*	*next year*
______	______	______
______	______	______
______	______	______
______	______	______

b) The past is over, the present is a fact or what is happening now and the future will happen at some time. Look at these sentences from Theme 1 and write them in your exercise book under the correct heading: the past, the present or the future.

Pete had lots more examples.

There are still many other orcas left in their small tanks.

You can test drugs on animals.

A film was made about the lives of whales in captivity.

Nothing will make me look beautiful.

An orca is one of the world's largest mammals.

I asked if the shampoo had been tested on animals.

Their wild relations will be lost forever.

Animal research has given humans many benefits.

New ingredients still have to be tested.

New technology means there are always new methods of testing.

I didn't want to hear them.

c) Use the verbs to make up six sentences of your own in the past, the present and the future.

B5 Tiger headlines

a) Use the reading record in WB B1 to write down the headlines of the five paragraphs in TB B3. Either use these ideas to help you or find your own.

Domestic cats and big cats

Cats in danger

Cats – big and small

The tigers are disappearing

Doctor Tiger

Tiger – a cure for everything

Save the tiger

It's not too late

No money for the hunters

b) Say in about one or two sentences what each paragraph is about.

B6 Under threat

Fill in the grid with the information from TB B3.

part	treatment for
brain	
whiskers	
teeth	
stomach	upset stomachs
blood	
tail	
fur	
flesh	
skin	mental diseases
bones	
eyes	epilepsy, malaria, nervousness in children

B7 Another way of saying it

Here is a list of words from TB B3.

beginning – change – dead – habitat – illegal – international – investigated – last – lost – most – next to – particularly – relations – roam – sickness – sold – support – traditions

a) Find words in the box above which mean the opposite of these:

1. bought ______________
2. first ______________
3. found ______________
4. end ______________
5. least ______________
6. alive ______________
7. modern ideas ______________
8. keep ______________

b) Find words in the box above which mean the same as these:

1. brother, mother, cousin ______________
2. beside ______________
3. environment ______________
4. wander ______________
5. worldwide ______________

illness ______________
especially ______________
4. looked into ______________
5. help ______________
6. not allowed ______________

B8 Adopt a tiger

Look at this advertisement from an English magazine.

a) Imagine you are one of the poachers[1]. Jasper's mother killed your only cow. Write a short account of your side of the story.

b) Imagine you are the environmentalist[2] who found Jasper. Write your version of the story.

c) Write a progress report – Jasper has escaped after six months.

d) Design a t-shirt logo for Jasper.

[1]poacher = *Wilderer;*
[2]environmentalist = *Umweltschützer*

[1]horribly = *fürchterlich;* [2]orphan = *zur Waise machen;* [3]fund = *finanziell unterstützen;* [4]renewal =*Verlängerung;* [5]donation = *Spende;* [6]foster parent = *Pflegeelternteil;* [7]postal order = *Geldgutschein, der bei der Post gekauft und eingelöst wird;* [8]debit = *belasten;* [9]expiry date = *Ablaufdatum*

Tigers suffer horribly[1] at the hands of poachers. The illegal tiger-bone industry for Chinese medicines is pushing the tiger to extinction. Adopting Jasper, who was orphaned[2] when poachers killed his mother, will help us to help him and fund[3] tiger protection projects worldwide.

For just £18.95 you'll receive a gift pack including:

- an adoption certificate with a colour picture of Jasper
- a history of Jasper's background • a tiger fact sheet
- an exclusive T-Shirt • a progress report after six months
- a renewal[4] request after twelve months

The pack is available individually (without a donation[5]) for £4.95

Care for the Wild International, I Ashfolds, Horsham Road, Rusper, West Sussex, RH12 4QX. Telephone (01293) 871596. Fax (01293) 871022. E-mail: info@careforthewild.com Web: http://www.careforthwild.com Registered charity no. 288802

SHE802

Yes! I would like to adopt Jasper the orphan tiger:

Person making payment	**Foster[6] parent**
Mr/Mrs/Miss/Ms	Mr/Mrs/Miss/Ms
Address	Address
Postcode	Postcode

Please send the initial gift pack to: The foster parent ❑ The person making payment ❑

T-Shirt size: Childs ❑ Small ❑ Medium ❑ Large ❑ X-Large ❑

I enclose a cheque/postal order[7] ❑ Please debit[8] my credit card (Details below) ❑

Visa/Amex/Mastercard No. ______/______/______/______

Expiry[9] Date ______ Extra donation £______ **Total £** ______

Fore more information about Care for the Wild International please tick here ❑

Going to extremes

A1 Shocking?

a) Look at the following list of adjectives. Which ones would you use to describe the punks in TB A1? You may use your dictionary.

aggressive, irresponsible, thoughtful, noisy, funny, cool, sensitive, dangerous, ridiculous, friendly, fascinating, stupid, creative, rebellious, intelligent, violent, shocking, peaceful

b) Write the adjectives in two lists, positive and negative.
Compare your lists with those of your classmates. Are they the same or are they different?

positive	negative

c) Do you know a person where more than four of your positive adjectives would fit?
Describe the person in some detail.

CD

A2 Tattooism today

Listen to the extract from a talk given by the owner of a tattoo studio in Manchester and answer the questions.

1. What is the code of conduct[1]?
2. Name two reasons why tattooists do not tattoo certain parts of the body.
3. When did the speaker open his studio?
4. How many studios are there now?
5. Who usually had tattoos?
6. What does a modern tattooist need?

[1]conduct = *Verhalten*

A3 Do it yourself

wbw 56

Fill in the missing self pronouns. Be careful – sometimes you don't need a pronoun!

1. Perry Farrell expresses __________________ in a very provocative way.
2. My grandmother speaks to __________________ all the time.
3. I saw the film __________________ some time ago.

   I remember __________________ it very well.
4. When the girl arrived at the corner she turned __________________ round and looked at me.
5. Let's enjoy __________________ and have something to drink.
6. Are you hungry? Help __________________ !
7. He doesn't know about it __________________, so he won't be able to tell you anything.
8. They must hurry __________________, or they'll be late.

A4 Your favourite sub-culture

Look at TB A3 again and at the lists you made. Which of the groups – they are also called sub-cultures – do you like best?

a) Use the words in your lists to write a short text about the sub-culture that you find most interesting. Here is some information to help you. You can find other information in the library or on the internet.

The '60s: Hippies
"Flower power" movement offered peace and love - protests against Vietnam War - rock music was not only about fun but also about political change - big festivals like Woodstock became important

The '70s: Punks
Rebelled against "hippy" rock business - looked poor and angry - dressed to shock - many punk rockers couldn't play their instruments - new energy brought to music

The '80s: Rappers
Started in the US - often texts spoken to music - talked about social problems such as gang wars, drugs, weapons, sexuality, fashion, problems of the poor - rappers imitated[1] street fights in their songs - music was like theatre

b) What about today's music? Can you write a summary similar to the ones above?

[1]imitate = *nachahmen*

A5 My style

In this theme, you have looked at different youth cultures and their styles.

What is YOUR style?
What sort of clothes do you like?
What hairstyles do you prefer?
What sort of music? Think about groups and the lyrics of their songs.
Do you belong to a sub-culture?
What do you think about the style of other young people?

Write a short text about yourself and explain what you like and why.

portfolio

A6 At your service

wbw 21

**a) Look at the advertisement in the Yellow Pages above.
Match up the services below with the names of the companies in the box.**

Bike Peddlers – Marc Saint – Max – Olympia

1. You can have flowers delivered by this company. ______________________

2. You can have your bike repaired by this company. ______________________

3. You can have your t-shirt printed by this company. ______________________

4. You can have a tattoo done by this company. ______________________

accessories = *Zubehör;* delivery = *Lieferung;* fruitless = *fruchtlos;* maintenance = *Wartung;* make = *Fabrikat;* manufacturer = *Hersteller*

b) Look at the ads again. Fill in the gaps to make sentences about the other companies. Use verbs from the box.

clean – deliver – do – repair

1. You can have your ________________ ________________ by Simpsons.
2. You can have ________________ ________________ by The Flower Gallery.
3. You can have ________________ ________________ by Jock's Studio.
4. You can have your ________________ ________________ by A1 Ltd.

B1 Doing the lemming

Can you match the expressions from TB B5 to the explanations?

1. Been there, done that
2. The location was really remote
3. had provided only
4. from where you could start this hopefully death-defying and doubtlessly ridiculous mission
5. do the lemming
6. they were quick and agile in their movements
7. it merely added to my discomfort
8. the margin for error is so small
9. there aren't really many parts to screw up
10. for the continued existence of their customers
11. I'm gonna lose my brains here
12. needless to say
13. to find the nerve to do it
14. my feeling was not one of fear but of weightlessness

a. for the safety of the people jumping
b. they moved easily and quickly
c. I wasn't afraid but I felt weightless
d. it only made me feel more uncomfortable[1]
e. the place was far away from any town or village
f. of course
g. there isn't much chance of making a mistake
h. rush over the edge of a canyon like lemmings
i. you can't make many mistakes
j. there was just
k. I'm going to die
l. that's finished now
m. have the courage to do it
n. where to begin this jump

[1]uncomfortable = *unbehaglich*

B2 In front of me, below me and behind me

In the following sentences the prepositions are missing. Fill them in. The text in TB B5 will help you.

wbw 47

1. The bungee jumper was standing ______________ an old bridge ______________ Queenstown.
2. He was ____________________ to do the most exciting thing ____________________ his life.
3. A towel and a nylon strip were tied ____________________ and __________________ his ankles.
4. There was only the empty canyon ________________ him, chilly air ________________ him and a so-called helper _______________________ him.
5. When he wanted to jump ____________________ the helper pulled him ____________________.
6. The next time the bungee jumper jumped ______________________ three.
7. Chilly air rushed ___________________ his ears.
8. The river ___________________ was suddenly very near.
9. The bungee caught him just a few feet _____________ the creek and shot him back _____________ the bridge.

B3 On the way

In, on **and** ***at*** **are three prepositions you need very often. Can you complete these expressions with the right preposition? Some of them have been taken from TB B5.**

wbw 47, 76

_______ three seconds	_______ that point
_______ an incredible speed	_______ their part
_______ the way	_______ summer
_______ the bridge	_______ four o'clock
_______ my life	_______ December
_______ the side	_______ Monday
_______ the evening	_______ the beach
_______ school	_______ morning
_______ the weekend	_______ home

wbw 48

B4 I have been there

Use the present perfect forms of these verbs to complete the sentences:

learn • be • wrap • jump • have • build • want

1. A.J. Hackett Bungy ____________ ____________ a wooden platform at the side of the bridge.
2. Thousands of people ____________ already ____________ from the bridge.
3. The helpers ____________ ____________ their job well.
4. The bungee jumper ____________ just ____________ a cotton towel round his ankles.
5. He ____________ never ____________ on that bridge before.
6. We ____________ ____________ enough time to think about the problem.
7. Men and women ____________ always ____________ to be able to fly.

B5 Bits of words

Use these syllables to find the words:

bot - can - chil - cot - en - ing - ly - ly - ly - lone - ment - move - no - ny - out - paint - quick - side - thrill - ti - tom - ton - where - wood - yon

1. made of wood ____________
2. opposite of inside ____________
3. it makes the walls of your room look nicer ____________
4. you can feel like this when nobody is around ____________
5. opposite of everywhere ____________
6. noun for move ____________
7. jeans are made of it ____________
8. a very narrow valley ____________
9. opposite of slowly ____________
10. another word for cold ____________
11. very small ____________
12. opposite of top ____________
13. a feeling of excitement ____________

B6 Hobbies can change

a) Do you still have the hobby / hobbies you had two or three years ago? What are your interests today?

81, 11, 85, 17, 72, 21

b) Write down questions you can ask one of your classmates about his / her hobbies. Be prepared to answer his / her questions as well.

What / your hobby? | this / your favourite hobby? | When / you do it?

What / other hobbies / you got? | How often / you do it? | you / train regularly?

How long / you / been doing this? | Why / you start it? | Who / give you / the idea?

it / expensive? | your parents / like your hobby?

c) Use the answers you got to write about your partner's hobby.

B7 How long?

a) Write down for how long or since when you have done something.

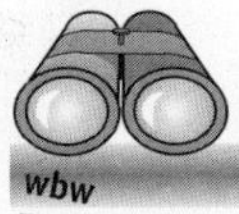

76, 48

learn English • ride a bike • play football / tennis / handball • play the piano / guitar / trumpet • go to school • smoke • listen to music • live in this place

I've played the guitar for two years.

b) Now write down for how long or since when you have had some of these things.

my computer • my bike • a TV set • my watch • my German teacher • my favourite t-shirt / CD / ring / earrings /... • my hair colour

I've had this hair colour since last month.

3 Red Power

A1 American Indians

a) Work with a partner and write down:

1. Five facts about the American Indians: things you are absolutely certain about.
2. Five questions you have about the American Indians: their history, their lifestyle, their present living conditions.

b) Together with your partner, find another pair to work with.

1. Look at their facts and compare them to yours. Are they the same or different? Do you agree they are facts?
2. Look at their questions and compare them to yours. Can you (at least partly) answer any of them?
3. Choose four facts that you are all certain about and four questions you all think worth answering. Each group member is given one fact and one question.
4. Can you prove that the facts are facts and find answers to the questions? Use different resources such as encyclopaedias etc., which you can find in a public library. Report your findings to the class.

A2 On the word path

tip
The phonetic transcriptions in your dictionary will help you.

/ˈgʌvənmənt/	/ɪgˈzɪstns/	/səˈsaɪəti/	/prəˈdʌktɪv/
/ˌedʒəˈkeɪʃn/	/ˈsɪvəlaɪzd/	/ˌbru:ˈtæləti/	/dɪsˈpeə/
/di:ˈɪndiənaɪz/	/nəˈsesəti/	/dɪsˈtrɔɪ/	/ˌmʌltiˈkʌltʃərəl/
/dɪˈzi:z/	/ɪˈstæblɪʃ/	/kəˈmju:nɪkeɪt/	

a) Find these words in TB A2 and write them down.

**b) Underline verbs, nouns and adjectives in different colours.
Make a list like this:**

civilize – civilized – civilization

What typical endings for nouns have you found? Do you know others?

c) Write the phonetic transcriptions of five more words from TB A2 and let your partner guess what they stand for.

d) Choose six words in TB A2 which you find most difficult and explain them in English.

e) Compare with your partner's choice.

A3 Lakota Woman's story

a) Read TB A3 in your textbook and say if these sentences are true (t), false (f) or not in the text (n)?

1. Lakota Woman thinks that even in good schools there is a cold atmosphere. ☐
2. Indian time is the same as the white man's time. ☐
3. Lakota Woman was taken to a modern school run by nuns. ☐
4. Boarding schools were opened to solve the Indian Problem. ☐
5. The kids were taken away by the government officials. ☐
6. Sometimes they were away for as long as two years. ☐
7. When they came back home they felt very unhappy. ☐
8. The mission school at St. Francis was a curse for Mary's family. ☐
9. Once her grandmother was kept in darkness for a week as punishment. ☐
10. The school is now run by the Bureau of Government Affairs. ☐
11. Mary hates and mistrusts every white person. ☐
12. She mentions that the only Lakota-English dictionaries and grammars were put together by two German fathers. ☐

b) Use these facts to write a summary of this extract. Remember you can use either the present or the past tense.

A4 Being civilized?

wbw 37, 8

a) Use these fragments and add the verb to write complete sentences.

Example: Mary – one of the better, modern schools.

Mary was not taken to one of the better, modern schools.

1. She – old-fashioned mission school.

____

2. Kids – from their villages and pueblos.

____

3. Kids – completely isolated from their families.

____

4. These kids – by whites or by Indians.

____

5. Kids who disobeyed – punished

____

6. Mary's grandmother – three other girls – found – brought back.

____

7. In the 1960s, the mission school – by the Church.

____

8. The only Lakota – English dictionary – together by them.

____

b) Underline the passive structures in your sentences.

A5 If I could...

wbw 12

portfolio

a) Write chain poems like this about yourself and other people you know. Make drafts.
b) Then try to improve them and discuss ideas with your neighbours.
c) Now publish your poems.
   Maybe you can set up a poetry corner in your classroom.

If I could *not watch my own TV,*
I would *be very unhappy.*
If I could ...,
I would ...

If my friend Peter could ...,
he would ...
But if he had to ...,
he wouldn't ...

A6 My point of view

Mary writes about her feelings at school. What would you write? Finish the sentences and compare with your neighbours.

1. All I get out of school is ______________________________

____

2. I do not take kindly to ______________________________

____

3. I was never one to like being forced to ______________________________

____

4. It has a bad effect on me when ______________________________

____

5. I can relate to and be friends with ______________________________

____

A7 Racial prejudice

The following text is from the American Indian Digest.
a) Try to explain in your own language what it says.
b) What do you think about this statement? Make notes and share your ideas with your class.

As man adapted[1] to his geographic environment, he developed certain physical characteristics[2], learned to walk upright[3], lost some body hair, and became a social creature. Tribal prejudice became a human instinct which is based on fear and was necessary for survival. Most human beings still have some degree[4] of tribal prejudice. People are most comfortable around people like themselves.
Racial[5] prejudice is a mutation[6] of tribal prejudice that evolved from fear to hate. When carried to the extreme, racial prejudice festers[7] into racism. Racism is learned and is generational. If the older folks would leave the kids alone, it will dissipate[8] very rapidly.
In today's society, human similarities are more important than racial differences.
Within the next two generations, racism as we know it will be a moot[10] issue. It's a waste of time on a foregone[11] conclusion.

[1]adapt = *sich anpassen;* [2]characteristics = *Merkmale;* [3]upright = *aufrecht;* [4]degree = *Maß;* [5]racial prejudice = *Rassenvorurteile;* [6]mutation = *Variante;* [7]fester = *sich auswuchern;* [8]dissipate = *sich auflösen;* [9]rapidly = *schnell;* [10]moot issue = *fragliche Sache;* [11]foregone conclusion = *eine Sache, die von vornherein feststeht.*

c) Check with various dictionaries – how do they explain "racism". How would you explain it?
d) Look for songs that deal with the problem and present them to your class (e.g. *Across the lines* by Tracy Chapman)

A8 Like cats – like dogs

An old Lakota medicine man compares his people with cats. Can you compare people you know with animals?

My friend ... is like a .... He / She can / can't .... He / She would ... when... .

If ... were an animal he / she would be a / an... because ...

3

wbw 9, 37, 16 24, 8

A9 Indian homes

a) Unscramble the following sentences and write them in your exercise book.

1. of Indian tribes / were built / The homes / in many different ways
2. the wind and snow / Homes / to keep out / in cold or even icy places / were built
3. to be / In warmer climate / were designed / as cool as possible / homes
4. homes / On swampy[1] ground / on stilts[2] / off the ground / were raised up
5. with little wood / were used / mud[3], brush[4] and sod[5] / In areas
6. houses / of planks[6] / an area with lots of wood, / In the Northwest / were made
7. Nomadic[7] tribes / and taken down /built homes / that could be put up
8. Animal hides[8] / as building material / were used / by Nomadic plain tribes

[1]swampy = *sumpfig*; [2]stilts = *Pfähle*; [3]mud = *Schlamm*; [4]brush = *Unterholz*; [5]sod = *Grassode*; [6]planks = *Bretter*; [7]nomadic = *nomadisch*; [8]hides = *Felle*

b) Match the pairs.

Pueblos were built
These houses were made of
Pueblos were often built
A pueblo roof was used
A wooden ladder[1] was used
When enemies attacked the town
The roof of the house was used

against the side of a mountain.
the ladder was taken inside.
by the Hopi who were farmers.
for household work, relaxing and sleeping.
as a door and to let out smoke.
stone or hard dried mud.
to reach the roof from outside.

[1]ladder = *Leiter*

c) The following sentences are not correct. Correct them using the passive form.

Example: Mohicans called their homes teepees.
I think you're wrong, their homes ***were called*** wigwams.

1. They made their homes with poles covered by animal hides.

   I'm afraid that's not true, their wigwams ____________________

   with poles covered by tree bark.

2. Algonquin Indians shaped[1] their wigwams like cones[2].

   Sorry, but that's not correct, their wigwams ____________________ like domes[3].

3. Woodland Indians set up cone-shaped wigwams for permanent use.

   Sorry, but I'm absolutely sure that their wigwams ____________________ for temporary use only.

4. Woodland Indians designed their wigwams with poles and animal hides.

   That's not quite true, those wigwams ____________________ with poles and bark.

5. The Sioux Nation used twenty-foot-long oak or maple[4] poles for their teepees.

   The fact is that twenty-foot-long cedar[5] or pine[6] poles ____________________ for the teepees of

   the Sioux Nation.

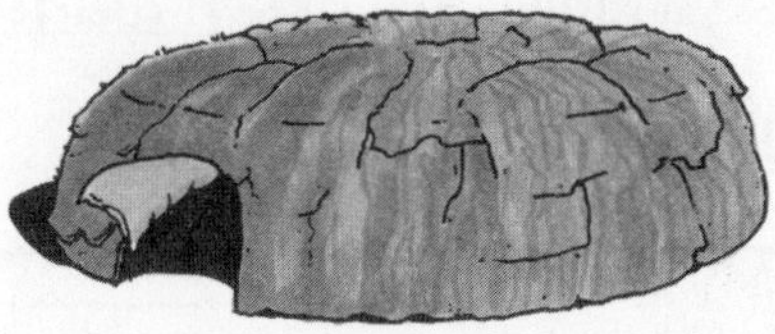

6. The Sioux Nation covered their tepees with horse hides.

   Actually their teepees ____________________ with buffalo hides.

[1]shape = *formen*; [2]cone = *Kegel*; [3]dome = *Kuppel*;
[4]maple = *Ahorn*; [5]cedar = *Zeder*; [6]pine = *Kiefer*

d) Fill in the gaps in the sentences below using the verb forms in the box.

were held • were conducted[1] • were protected • was made up • was constantly kept burning • was surrounded[2] • was constructed • were usually built • were often spent • were all similarly arranged[3] • were plastered[4]

The Cherokee inhabited[5] mountains and valleys in the southeast of North America. The Cherokee Nation ____ of numerous[6] Indian villages. The villages ____ near rivers and streams. They____________ ____. In the center stood the Council House where important meetings ____. Celebrations, ceremonial dances and public games ____ on "the Square" near the Council House.

Around the village stood a stockade[7]. It ______________________ from tall wooden posts[8]. Here the Cherokee ______________________ against surprise attacks. The village ______________________ by the homes of the Cherokee families. These homes ______________________ with a mixture of clay and grass. They had no windows. Cold winter nights ______________________ in a hothouse, a small earth-covered dugout[9] nearby. A fire ______________________ ______________ within a hothouse[10] for warmth. Special ceremonies also took place in the hothouse[10].

[1]conduct = *führen*; [2]surround = *umgeben*; [3]arrange = *anlegen*; [4]plaster = *verputzen*; [5]inhabit = *bewohnen*; [6]numerous = *zahlreich*; [7]stockade = *Palisade*; [8]post = *Pfosten*; [9]dugout = *Unterschlupf*; [10]hothouse = *Treibhaus*

A10 Homes across the world

Now you know a lot about Indian homes. Find out about other peoples' homes and describe them using passive structures.

wbw 37, 8

Example:

Skyscrapers *are often made of concrete and glass.*

Igloos ______________________

My dream house ______________________

wbw
77, 59

B1 How to behave

a) Unscramble the following sentences:

1. to be / want / hospitable / their people / American Indians

____

2. to follow / a guest / expect / their customs / They

____

3. merciful / tell / in their power / They / to be / their children / to those

____

4. not / the poisonous firewater / They / their people / to touch / ask

____

5. to preserve / They / hope / of their land / the beauty / to be able

____

6. why / That is / to clean up / want / people / all the rubbish / they

____

b) What do your parents want you to do or not to do? Write sentences and collect all your ideas. What do you think is important and / or acceptable? Discuss in groups.

My parents want me to _______________

They expect me to _______________

They often tell me to _______________

____

____

____

____

____

____

c) What do you expect your best friend to do and not to do? Write two sentences.

____

____

d) Compare with your neighbour and report to the class. You may start like this:

I would never expect my best friend to …

My neighbour expects his best friend to…

My neighbour and I expect our best friends to …

B2 Pocahontas – what's in a song?

Are these sentences true (t), false (f) or not in the text (n)?

1. Pocahontas cannot accept that she is the savage. ☐
2. She knows the name of every person of her people. ☐
3. She asks if the white man has ever killed a grinning bobcat. ☐
4. She asks if the white man can run the hidden trails of the forest. ☐
5. She asks if the white man has ever tasted the sun-sweet berries. ☐
6. She says all the animals are her friends. ☐
7. She thinks it is wrong to cut the sycamore. ☐
8. She wants white and copper-skinned people to respect nature. ☐

B3 Nature words

a) Collect all the nature words from the song lyrics and write them down here.

____

____

____

____

portfolio

b) Use these words to write a poem like this two-word poem, for example:

Indian nature

sun-sweet berries

grinning bobcats

running rivers

c) Draw a picture that goes with the song or your poem and make an exhibition in your school.

B4 The Cherokee reservation

Read TB B7 and match up these sentence halves.

1. The Cherokee welcome visitors
2. Their traditions enable them
3. The Cherokee reservation has all the attractions it takes
4. They ask their visitors
5. They expect the tourists who enjoy fishing
6. Cherokee craftsmen want tourists

a. to make a fun-filled family vacation.
b. to buy head-dresses and moccasins.
c. to see a compelling outdoor drama.
d. to find out more about their land.
e. to buy a daily tribal fishing permit.
f. to live in harmony with nature.

B5 Indian associations

a) Work with your partner. Fill in an answer to each question below in the column I think of ... Then find a partner and ask him / her. How many of your answers were the same?

What do you think of when you hear the word... ?	I think of	My partner thinks of
reservations	__________	__________
festivals	__________	__________
souvenirs	__________	__________
nature	__________	__________
tribes	__________	__________
paradise	__________	__________
traditions	__________	__________

b) Talk to other pairs and the whole class. What do you agree about most? Use the following phrases:

That's interesting/strange/ surprising because ...

My partner and I think of... What about you?

c) Write your favourite associations into your exercise book and use them to write a text about American Indians. Publish it in class.

B6 Indian language in English

In the following text some words have been left out. Choose words from the list below and put them where they belong.

Cheyenne – colonists – difficult – easier – English – hammock[1] – maize[2] – Mississippi – moccasin – names – American Indians – objects – Pawnee – plants – racoon[3] – toboggan[4] – tomahawk – United States – words

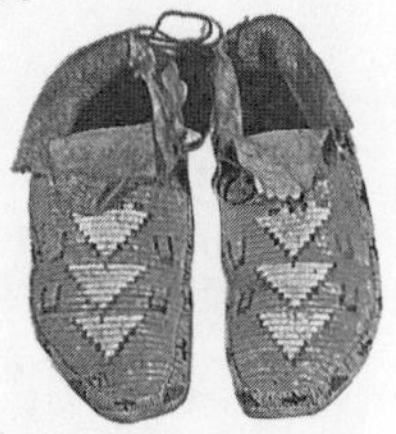

Before the arrival of the __________ from Europe, there were about two million native Americans living in what later became the __________. There were about six major groups living in different areas. For example the plains in the centre were the homelands of several tribes such as the __________ and the __________.
Many European colonists were unable to identify a lot of the __________, animals and __________ which they saw in the New World. So words from the languages of the American Indians were integrated into the __________ language. Words such as __________ for the natives' soft shoes and __________ for a light axe[5], later on __________ for the vehicle[6] used to slide[7] over the snow or __________ for a "bed" which can be hung up and __________ for a cereal[8] were all originally American Indian words for which the settlers[9] had no English words.

Many animals in America today are named after words first heard from ____________________ .
Of course, the way a word was spelt or pronounced[10] was sometimes too ____________________
for English tongues and so the words were changed to make them ____________________ : for example, the name ____________________ , for a small furry[11] animal, came from the native word raugraughcum, to much of a tongue-twister for the English speakers.
In all, about 250–300 ______________ found their way into the English language. But perhaps the longest are the ________________ which the native Americans gave to places: names such as Monongahela or ____________________________ which have a very poetic[13] ring[14] to them.

[1]hammock = *Hängematte*; [2]maize = *Mais*; [3]racoon = *Waschbär*; [4]toboggan = *Schlitten*; [5]axe = *Axt*; [6]vehicle = *Fahrzeug*
[7]slide = *rutschen*; [8]cereal = *Getreideart*; [9]settlers = *Siedler*; [10]pronounce = *aussprechen;* [11]furry animal = *Pelztier;*
[12]tongue-twister = *Zungenbrecher*; [13]poetic = *poetisch*; [14]have a ring = *klingen*

tip
Look at the maps of the USA on the insides of the cover of your TB.

B7 Little known facts

Did you know that the names of over half of the states in the USA came from American Indian languages?
For example UTAH is the Ute tribe's name for themselves in their language. OKLAHOMA means RED PEOPLE in the Choctaw language, KENTUCKY means planted field in the Iroquois language. TEXAS means friend.

a) In this word grid you can find the names of 24 US states with Indian names. The remaining letters name the 25th state and an Indian tribe.

A	L	A	S	K	A	N	I	S	N	O	C	S	I	W
T	C	I	O	W	A	A	K	E	N	T	U	C	K	Y
O	O	L	U	A	B	N	A	G	I	H	C	I	M	O
S	N	S	T	T	E	S	U	H	C	A	S	S	A	M
E	N	A	H	S	A	S	N	A	K	R	A	I	M	I
N	E	W		M	E	X	I	C	O	I	S	L	I	N
N	C	O	D	K	A	N	S	A	S	Z	A	L	S	G
I	T	H	A	H	A	T	U	M	A	O	X	I	S	O
M	I	A	K	S	A	R	B	E	N	N	E	N	O	I
H	C	D	O	K	L	A	H	O	M	A	T	O	U	H
O	U	I	T	E	N	N	E	S	S	E	E	I	R	O
P	T	I	A	I	P	P	I	S	S	I	S	S	I	M

b) Can you also find out what they mean? What about searching the Internet?
c) Some of these names are difficult to pronounce. Use a dictionary and check.

War – and peace

A1 Better interviewing

Unfortunately, your interview partner is rather reluctant or shy. He or she gives only short answers or can hardly remember:

1. You: Where did you live at the beginning of the war?
   Interviewee: In London.
2. You: Did you live there with your family?
   Interviewee: Yes, yes.
3. You: What details do you remember?
   Interviewee: Not too many, I'm afraid.
4. You: What did you see or hear?
   Interviewee: It was awful.

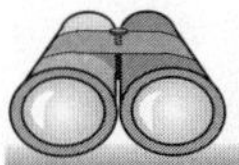

a) How could you ask follow-up questions and get him or her to say more?

1. ______________________________

2. ______________________________

3. ______________________________

4. ______________________________

b) Now write down more questions which allow the interviewee to answer in more than one word. You could ask about public transport, food, family life or free time activities.

____

____

____

____

____

____

____

____

A2 Mrs Haggarty's war

a) Listen to the interview two students from Holland Park School recorded with Mrs Haggarty about her war experiences. Decide whether the statements are true (t), false (f) or if no information is given in the recording (n).

CD

Part I	T	F	N
1. The girl asks Mrs Haggarty to speak naturally.			
2. Mrs Haggarty was ten when war was declared.			
3. When war was declared, Mrs Haggarty was evacuated to Guernsey.			
4. Mrs Haggarty was scared when she heard the Prime Minister's declaration of war on the radio.			
5. After the German invasion of France, it was decided to evacuate all school children from the Channel Islands.			
6. That was the first time that Mrs Haggarty had lived away from her parents.			
7. She had both positive and negative feelings about evacuation.			
Part 2			
8. The Germans, in fact, did not invade the Channel Islands.			
9. The evacuees travelled with their teachers by plane and train from Guernsey to Patricoft, near Manchester.			
10. They all first had to sleep in a church hall.			
11. Mrs Haggarty didn't like her host family.			
12. The evacuees had lessons in a local school.			
13. The last air raid which Mrs Haggarty experienced was in the winter of 1941.			
14. One of her most lasting memories is of the air raid sirens.			

b) Listen to the interview again and note down Mrs Haggarty's feelings about being evacuated and about the air raids. Make two lists, one with positive, one with negative feelings.

A3 What did they ask?

wbw 81, 85, 55

Look at TB A4 and write down the first questions for each of the twelve interviews.

1. *What did you do when you heard that war had been declared?*
2. ______________________________
3. ______________________________
4. ______________________________
5. ______________________________

6a. ______________________________

6b. ______________________________

7. ______________________________

8. ______________________________

9. ______________________________

10. ______________________________

11. ______________________________

12. ______________________________

A4 Explain what it really is

a) Mark the correct meaning of these words. If necessary, use your dictionary.

1. *Civilians* are ...
   a. people who work for the state.
   b. people who are not members of the armed forces.
   c. polite and friendly people.

2. When children are *evacuated* they are ...
   a. sent to a safe place.
   b. sent home from school.
   c. punished.

3. *Declare* war means ...
   a. to explain what a *war* really is.
   b. to begin a war.
   c. to state that war now officially exists.

4. *ID* card is in German ...
   a. **I**nternationales **D**okument.
   b. Personalausweis.
   c. Computerlaufwerk. *(Internal Drive)*

5. An *air raid* is ...
   a. a battle in the air.
   b. an air crash.
   c. an attack by aircraft.

6. The women in the *Women's Voluntary Service* ...
   a. worked freely in a company.
   b. worked to be trained for a special job.
   c. helped the civilians during the war.

7. *Blackout* is ...
   a. a period in wartime when a place is made completely dark.
   b. a meeting for whites only.
   c. a card game.

8. When you are looking for *shelter* ...
   a. you want to find something to eat or drink.
   b. you want to find protection.
   c. you want to earn money.

9. *Enemy* is the opposite of ...
   a. human being.
   b. partner.
   c. friend.

10. *First aid* is ...
    a. the beginning of a bad illness.
    b. first medical help before a doctor comes.
    c. money to help to start up a business.

b) Find more examples of words in the texts. Use your dictionary to make up tests for your friends.

A5 Build – builder – building

Have a look at text 7 in TB A4 and find the four nouns which are derived from other words by adding a new ending (*suffix*).

wbw 83

a) Write the words down in the following list and add the original word in brackets.

-er	boarders (board)
-ment	
-ing	
-ist	

b) Now think of at least three more examples of *noun* suffixes and add them to the list.

A6 Memories of the Blitz

CD

There are two statements about the war on tape only. Every fifth word has been removed. Listen to the statements and fill in the gaps. If you like, you might also take a few guesses before you start listening.

1. On one occasion during _________ Blitz we had had _________ bad night and I _________ in a bus, trying _________ get to Bexley Heath _________ Kent. Because of unexploded _____________ we were going down _____________ streets. Two young boys _____________ on the bus and _________ conductor[1] said, "What are _________ doing back in London? ___________ should have stayed evacuated." ___________ reply was: "Blimey, they're _______________ them to buggery[2] down ___________ ." You couldn't give an _____________ to that, only realize ___________ to them, no matter[3] ___________ , home still seemed safer.

2. Our wartime memories are _________ odd mixture of the _____________ and the harrowing[4], but _________ give an idea of _________ odd times in which ___________ were all living. Blackout _________ something unforgettable especially when _____________ with fog or smog: _____________ off from trams and _____________ required both nerve and _____________ ! Some nights I spent _________ First Aid duty in _________ basement of the largest _________________ store in Leeds – I _________ don't know why, as ___________ were no staff in _________ store! One night in ___________ or 1944 we thought _________ were having an air ___________ in Leeds without any _____________ . It turned out to _________ a small earthquake[5]!

[1]conductor = *Schaffner;* [2]bomb to buggery = *in Grund und Boden bombardieren;* [3]no matter what = *egal was passiert;* [4]harrowing = *grauenhaft;* [5]earthquake = *Erdbeben*

A7 Words on war

Read the poems in TB A12. Do at least three of the following tasks.

1. **Learn one or more of the poems by heart and recite them in good English.**
2. **Who do you think is talking in the poems? Give reasons.**

   "Sheila carries ...": ____________________

   "War:" ____________________

   "When they sound ...": ____________________

3. **Which is the most, which is the least hopeful of the poems?**

   ____

   ____

   ____

4. **Invent a melody for "When they sound the last all-clear".**
5. **Draw simple pictures or find illustrations for the poems.**
6. **Collect "war" words from the poems.**

   ____

   ____

   ____

7. **Translate one of the poems into German.**

   ____

   ____

   ____

   ____

   ____

   ____

   ____

   ____

   ____

   ____

8. **Make up your own task and do it.**

A8 War is ...

a) Read the poem and answer the questions in your exercise book.

BOURNEMOUTH, SEPTEMBER 3rd, 1939

My summer ends, and term begins next week.
Why am I here in Bournemouth, with my aunt
And "Uncle Bill", who something tells me can't
Be really my uncle? People speak
In hushed[1], excited tones. Down on the beach
An aeroplane comes in low over the sea
And there's a scattering[2] as people reach
For towels and picnic gear[3] and books, and flee[4]
Towards the esplanade[5]. Back at the hotel
We hear what the Prime Minister has said.
"So it's begun." "Yes, it was bound[6] to." "Well,
Give it till Christmas." Later, tucked[7] in bed,
I hear the safe sea roll and wipe[8] away
The castles[9] I had built in sand that day.

Anthony Thwaite

1. Can you answer the poet's question beginning in line two?
2. Why do the people flee from the beach?
3. What has begun?
4. Why does the poet write about the destruction of sand castles?
5. How do we know this is a war poem?

[1]hushed tones = *mit gedämpfter Stimme;* [2]scattering = *Zerstreuung;* [3]gear = *Sachen, Zeug;* [4]flee = *flüchten;* [5]esplanade = *Strandpromenade;* [6]it was bound to (begin) = *es mußte beginnen;* [7]tucked = *zugedeckt;* [8]wipe away = *wegwischen;* [9]castle = *Burg*

b) Now write a collective war poem in class. Write short statements beginning "War is ..." on small slips of paper and combine them into a poem with a message.

War is killing.

War is the end of ...

War is no ...

B1 Consequences

wbw 37, 80

Find all the passive sentences in TB B2 und B4 and write them down in short form.

a point of view could be applied ...

wbw
77, 25

B2 What would people like them to do?

Write complete sentences to say what people want other people to do.

Richard Brooke / want / think of his grave.

Richard Brooke wants us to think of his grave.

1. The German War Graves Commission / want / young people work together.

____

2. The Commission / help / youths come together.

____

3. They / expect / nations live peacefully together.

____

4. Young people from Staffordshire / help / the German guests repair and tidy graves.

____

5. They / hope / nations never again go to war.

____

6. The local people / invite / Germans meet in clubs and in their own homes.

____

B3 The War Graves Commission's aims

Match the sentence halves.

1. The German War Graves Commission want German war graves abroad
2. They want to promote young people
3. They expect visitors
4. In the last few years 190 cemeteries in the former Eastern bloc
5. The Commission wants the memory of the war dead

a. had to be rebuilt.
b. to come together.
c. to be registered and cared for.
d. to be kept alive.
e. to be confronted with the consequences of war and violence.

1.	2.	3.	4.	5.

B4 Peace words

peace love happy charity life festivities liberty
reconciliation live humanitarian friends good safety human
understanding partner flowers dialogue joy peaceful friendship
help calm[1] play silence laughter Olympic Games beautiful

Look at these "peace words" for 30 seconds.

- **Then shut your workbook and write down as many words as you can remember.**
- **Compare with your neighbour and add your neighbour's words to your list.**
- **Check the spelling and the meaning of your words.**
- **Choose the words you find most important and explain them to your class OR collect the most important words in your class OR make a mind map with one of the most important words and present it to the class.**
- **Write a text with your partner.**

[1]calm = *ruhig*

B5 What will they remember?

Look at TB B6 again. What do you think will the young people remember?

Arek Koszek will keep the wonderful time deep in his memory.

He will remember ______________________________

Heidi will think of ______________________________

She will remember that they were ______________________________

____

____

____

____

____

____

____

____

____

Portfolio

Zum

ENGLISCHLERNEN

ist/sind für mich wichtig:

	Ja	Nein		Ja	Nein
Vokabeln	○	○	Lernspiele	○	○
Texte lesen	○	○	Dialoge	○	○
Geschichten schreiben	○	○	Tests	○	○
Geschichten hören	○	○	Lieder	○	○
Auswendiglernen	○	○	Aussprache	○	○
Computerübungen	○	○	Diskussionen	○	○
Grammatik	○	○	Hören	○	○
Landeskunde	○	○	Schreiben	○	○
Projekte	○	○	Übersetzen	○	○
Videos	○	○	____________	○	○

Was ich jetzt kann:

SCHREIBEN

	Kein Problem.	Ich mache ein paar Fehler.	Das muss ich noch üben.
Ich kann mir zu einem Thema Notizen machen.	○	○	○
Ich kann kurze Texte über mich schreiben.	○	○	○
Ich kann einfache Gedichte schreiben.	○	○	○
Ich kann mit einfachen Sätzen über ein Ereignis berichten.	○	○	○
Ich kann kurze persönliche Briefe schreiben.	○	○	○
Ich kann die Ergebnisse eines Projekts schriftlich darstellen.	○	○	○
Ich kann das Wichtigste aus einem Text schriftlich zusammenfassen.	○	○	○
Ich kann eine Geschichte schreiben.	○	○	○

portfolio

Was ich jetzt kann: **SPRECHEN**	Kein Problem.	Ich mache ein paar Fehler.	Das muss ich noch üben.
Ich kann etwas mithilfe von Notizen sagen.	○	○	○
Ich kann mich zu Bildern äußern.	○	○	○
Ich kann den Inhalt einer Geschichte oder eines Films kurz wiedergeben.	○	○	○
Ich kann anderen über eigene Erlebnisse berichten.	○	○	○
Ich kann über meine Träume, Hoffnungen und Ängste erzählen.	○	○	○
Ich kann meine Meinung zu einem Problem äußern.	○	○	○
Ich kann eine Interview durchführen.	○	○	○
Ich kann erklären, wie etwas funktioniert.	○	○	○

Wie ich lerne: **VOKABELN**	Kein Problem.	Ich mache ein paar Fehler.	Das muss ich noch üben.
Ich kann Wörter im Vokabelanhang des TB nachschlagen.	○	○	○
Ich kann ein Wörterbuch benutzen.	○	○	○
Ich kann unbekannte Wörter in einem Text erraten.	○	○	○
Ich kann mir Ersatzwörter ausdenken, wenn mir ein Wort nicht gleich einfällt.	○	○	○
Ich kann mir neue Wörter gut merken.	○	○	○

Ich lerne neue Wörter am besten

- ○ aus dem Buch.
- ○ wenn ich sie der Reihe nach aufschreibe.
- ○ wenn ich sie auf Kärtchen schreibe.
- ○ mit Wortfeldern und Wortnetzen.
- ○ wenn mich jemand abfragt.
- ○ wenn ich sie in Texten benutze.
- ○ ______________________

Freedom of speech

A1 Match the summaries

Here are some short summaries for each of the paragraphs in TB A1. Can you fill in the correct title next to each summary? One summary is missing – so you'll need to write your own summary for that paragraph.

SUMMARY	TITLE
Radiation risks from mobiles are greater for children.	
Radiation from mobiles can keep you awake at night.	
Text messaging can help kids with their reading and writing.	
You get more radiation from newer mobiles because you hold them nearer to your head.	
Kids smoke less because they need money for calls.	
Using mobile phones at the wrong time or place can be annoying or dangerous.	
Mobiles are used to show the user's lifestyle	

A2 YOUR view

Read Sophie's letter in TB A3. Write a letter or e-mail in reply, giving your own views about mobile phones. Do you accept the risks, or would you rather spend your money on something else?

If you like, you can use some of these phrases:

Dear Sophie, / Hi Sophie!

I think you're too negative about ...

I find it very practical to ...

In emergencies[1] mobile phones can ...

I don't agree that ...

Don't you think ...?

I can't imagine ...

You're right about ...

I totally agree with you that ...

It's too much to say that ...

Best wishes / Yours / Greetings

In my opinion ...

Although ..., you mustn't forget that ...

[1]emergency = *Notfall*

A3 Tell her goodbye

Look at the "Sylvia's mother" lyrics in TB A5 and decide whether these statements are true, false or "no information given":

	true	false	no info
1. The caller is trying to speak to Sylvia.	☐	☐	☐
2. Sylvia's mother doesn't want the caller to speak to Sylvia.	☐	☐	☐
3. Sylvia's new lover is called Galveston.	☐	☐	☐
4. Sylvia's new lover is older than the caller.	☐	☐	☐
5. Sylvia is going to marry her new lover.	☐	☐	☐
6. Sylvia's mother has forbidden her to see the caller.	☐	☐	☐
7. Sylvia would prefer to marry the caller.	☐	☐	☐
8. The caller is in love with Sylvia's mother.	☐	☐	☐

A4 The wonders of modern telecommunications!

Read the text of the song "Off the hook" in TB A6. Imagine you're the frustrated caller. Fortunately, you at least have the possibility to leave an answerphone or voicemail message for your "baby". Or maybe you'd like to try an SMS? What would you say or write?

If you're feeling really creative, why not re-write the whole song to bring it up to date?

tip

If this is all new to you, have a look at page 140 in your textbook for help.

pcm

khuf

SWDYT

bbfn

cul

CD

A5 Speak after the bleep!

Listen to the answer phone texts on the CD and make notes.

Text 1: Brecon Tourist Information: *What would you do if you were in a hurry?*

____

Text 2: Easyjet, the lowcost airline: *What's the Easyjet website for online reservations?*

____

Text 3: Virgin Records: *When are the helplines open?*

____

Text 4: Castleton Youth Hostel: *What's the phone number for bookings after 25 May?*

____

Text 5: Apollo Multiplex Cinema: *What do you do if you want to know which films are showing tomorrow?*

____

A6 Your own answer phone text

Work out your own answerphone text. Record it and play it to the class. Whose text did you find the clearest / most amusing / most creative?

A7 Give me a ring

Look at the telephone language below. Put the phrases into two lists: which phrases does a person use who is calling someone? Which ones does a person use who is being called?

Hello, is that … ?
I'm afraid he / she isn't in.
So sorry, I've got the wrong number.
Can she call you back? What's your number?
Hello, this is … from …
I couldn't call earlier because your line was engaged[1] / busy.
I'll just find out if he / she is in.
Could you ask … to call me back, please? My number is …
Sorry, my phone was out of order.
Good afternoon. I'd like to speak to …
Hold on a moment, please.
Is … in?
… speaking.
Could you give … a message, please?
Can I speak to …, please?
I'll put[2] you through to (him / her).

tip

Look at pages 139-140 in your TB for help.

[1]engaged = *besetzt;* [2]put s.o. through = *jn. verbinden*

A8 Just a minute

a) You are calling English-speaking people. But you can only get the answer phone. What do you say? Remember: you should be friendly and precise – there is only one minute for your message. Do not forget your name and your phone number or your address where needed.

tip

Look at pages 139-140 in your TB for help.

1. You want materials about Scotland from the Scottish Tourist Board for Theme 7 in NOTTING HILL GATE.

2. You have a problem with your English homework and want help from an English friend.

3. You are on your way to visit your penpal in Australia. There is a stopover in Hong Kong. You learn that the plane to Australia will be four hours late.

4. You want to invite your penpal in Sweden to stay at your house for two weeks.

5. **Your rich aunt and uncle invite you to a journey to India. You call the Embassy to find out about formalities (visa, vaccination[1], customs).**

6. **Your teacher asked you to get information from the *English Speaking Theatre:* programme, price of the tickets for the whole class, beginning and end of the performance.**

[1]vaccination = *Impfung*

b) Why not record the messages on tape?

A9 Thanks for calling

Listen to the cassette and find the correct answers. Write the numbers into the boxes.

1. It's a very bad line. Could you call me back, or shall I call you back? ☐
2. Don't worry. I'll be there in a minute. ☐
3. Wait a minute, I'll just check up for you. ☐
4. I'm sorry, I didn't quite get that. Could you speak more slowly, please? ☐
5. Hello. Who's speaking please? ☐
6. I'm sorry, I didn't quite catch your name. Could you spell it, please? ☐
7. That's very kind of you. Thanks for calling. ☐
8. Sorry, I prefer not to buy anything over the telephone. ☐

CD

tip

Look at pages 139-140 in your TB for help.

A10 Give us an answer!

wbw 24, 16, 81

a) Look at the information in the diagram. Fill in the empty spaces first and write questions and answers in your exercise book:

	Mike offered . . .	**Mary gave . . .**	**Sven sent . . .**	**Charlie lent . . .**	**Sarah bought . . .**
Bill	a new job.	an aftershave.	an e-mail.	a Rolling Stones CD.	an ice cream.
Nicola	a new PC.	a calculator.		his mountain bike.	a Chinese meal.
Barbara	a company car.				

Example: *What did Mike offer Bill? – He offered him a new job.*

wbw 24, 16, 20

b) Write about what you're going to give / buy / send / make your family and friends for their birthday / Christmas.

Example: *I'm going to make my mum a new pullover.*

B1 Teen talk

There are quite a few words or phrases in TB B1 which are fairly typical of British teenagers' talk.
Find six examples from the text which could be paraphrased in the following way:

spend a lot of time with	
fairly strong, explicit language	
boys we find sexy	
weak, not very shocking	
make a big mistake	
attack someone verbally	

B2 It's easy to say afterwards!

a) Read these comments people can make about other people's behaviour:

You shouldn't have said that. (= It was wrong of you to say that.)
You should have kept quiet. (= It would have been better to keep quiet.)
You needn't have done that. (= You did something which wasn't necessary.)
You could have practised more before the exam. (= Why didn't you practise more …?)

wbw
65, 33, 21

Now re-write the following critical comments, using *should have done* and similar modal verb phrases as above:

1. It was totally unnecessary to spy on my e-mails! (Use needn't …)
2. Instead of spying on me, why didn't you ask me who I'm hanging around with? (Use could …)
3. It was terrible of Jo's dad to bug her phone. (Use shouldn't …)
4. It's a pity her dad didn't trust her more. (Use should …)
5. Why didn't he speak to her before doing something terrible like that?
6. There was nothing to stop him speaking to his daughter first.
7. It was totally unnecessary to do something like that!
8. I'm sure Jo was pretty angry with him when she found out. (Use must …)

b) Now make some comments of your own about the kids and parents in TB B1. Say what they should have / shouldn't have / could have / needn't have done.

B3 Give it a title!

a) Read TB B5 again. Which paragraphs could you give the following titles?

How to send texts?

The invention of paper

b) Think of a suitable short title for each of the other paragraphs.

B4 Find the passives!

Write down all the passive verbs in TB B5:

wbw 37, 80

1. *would be used*
2. …

Which examples give the doer (Urheber) of the action by means of a phrase with *by*? Which do not?

B5 Pros and cons

a) Explain the advantages and disadvantages of these ways of sending messages:

- telephone
- fax
- e-mail
- letter
- SMS

b) In which situations would you prefer to use which?

B6 Passives

Put passive verbs into these jokes:

wbw 37, 8

1. Customer: Waiter, I'm sorry to complain, but there's a dead fly in my soup.

   Waiter: Yes, sir. I'm afraid it ____________________ (kill) by the heat.

2. Old lady: Do you go to school?

   Little boy: No, I ____________________ (send).

3. 25 year-old boy: I ____________________ (ask) to get married thousands of times.

   Female colleague: Really? Who by?

   Boy: My parents.

4. Little boy: Mummy, do all fairy[1] tales begin with "Once upon a time".

   Mother: No, dear. Some start with: "So sorry I'm late, darling. I ____________________

   (delay) at the office."

[1]fairy tale = *Märchen*

B7 Communication crossword

1. Kind of magazine for selling things
2. Phone you can take with you
3. Way of text messaging
4. Information which is sent to someone
5. People watching a film
6. Machine for leaving phone messages
7. A place on the Internet
8. A computer file
9. For listening to a phone or walkman
10. For making audio recordings
11. Electronic letter
12. Something you can hear
13. www

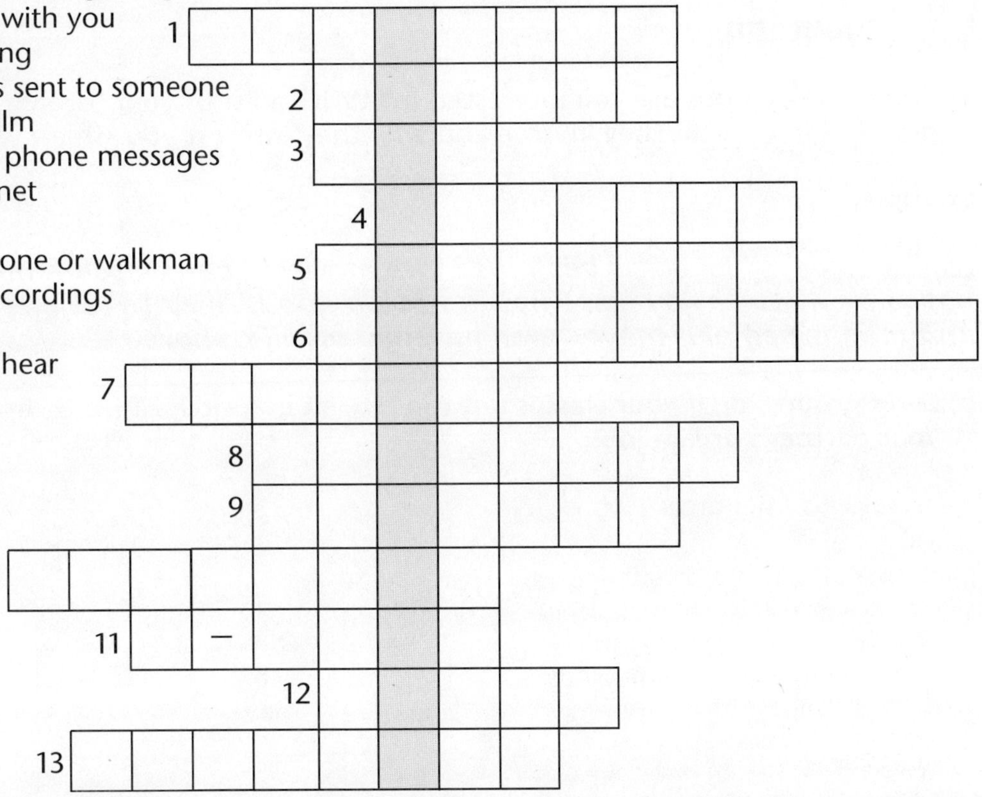

Why not make your own crossword based on the article "Are your parents spying on you?" Get together with a classmate! When you've finished, make copies for the rest of the class to try.

B8 In the next ten years

wbw 75, 82, 33

Now that you have read about the development of communication, what do you think it will be like in five or ten years time? How soon will things happen?

I think I expect I hope I reckon	there will be mobile TV phones we'll have ... there might be ... we may have ...	in	ten years time. five years time. the next ten years.

I don't think I doubt	there will be mobile TV phones we'll have ... there'll be ...	in	ten years time. five years time. the next ten years.
		for a long time yet.	

6 Let's work!

A1 Dream job

a) What kinds of jobs are you interested in? Write a list of your "dream" jobs and a short description of what they involve and why they interest you. Share with a partner.

Example:

I'd like to be a film critic because I love movies. I can watch films all day and take notes on what I enjoy and what is not so good. I'll write reviews for newspapers and magazines and maybe even have my own TV show.

b) Form groups, or, if your class is not too big, sit in a circle. Take turns and report about your partner's dream jobs.

wbw 60

… says his / her dream job is … .

He She	thinks imagines hopes …	he she	can will may	…	all day. most of the time. every now and then. some day. …

c) What kind of job would be awful for you? Tell your partner / group / class:

I don't think I	could ever 'd like to 'd be able to	be work as a(n) operate instruct advise …	…

A2 What's my job?

a) Listen to the CD. Make a note of how many questions the team members ask.

They ask __________ questions.

b) Listen to the CD again and make a note of the key word in each question. Then write out the questions in full.

inside *Do you work inside?*

c) What do you think Peter's job is? ______________________

d) Work in groups of six. You are going to play "What's my job?" Take it in turns to be the competitor, the team members and the presenter. Listen to the beginning of the CD again if you need to be reminded of the rules.

A3 Technically speaking

Find out from Steven's report in TB A2 what these words are in English. The number in brackets tells you which letter(s) to pick from the English word you've found.
Read TB A2 and write the letter(s) on the right margin and read them downwards to find the solution. The solution tells you what you should look for to improve your English.

Gegenbesuch (2): r(e)turn visit ______ E

Ausgaben (2): ______ ______

Berufsschulsystem (12, 13): ______ ______

KFZ-Auszubildender (1): ______ ______

Metallmutter (1): ______ ______

Schweißen (7): ______ ______

Hydraulik (14): ______ ______

Werkstatt (8): ______ ______

Firma (3): ______ ______

Fabrik (5): ______ ______

Ausland (6, 13): ______ ______

Fahrgestell (3): ______ ______

Unterkunft (5, 6): ______ ______

erklären (1): ______ ______

A4 Get it wrong?

CD

Read the report below. Somebody got something wrong here. Listen to Philippa Barnes again and cross out the incorrect information given in the report. Write the correct information above what you have crossed out.

Philippa Barnes is a teenager from ~~Dallas, Texas.~~ England When she got good results in her exams, she had to change her plans. Everybody tried to help her, but she really did not know what to do. After some temporary work, Philippa eventually[1] decided to go to Europe.

She had to write a couple of letters before she found something. It was a Camphill School in Southern France that offered her a job for three months. When Philippa arrived she spoke little French and had no idea of the culture or what to expect.

She really had to work a lot, but she loved being with the children and helping them. And doing so, she also helped herself: she spoke the language much better and gained self-confidence[2] again.

Now Philippa is back home in the States. She is going to look for a chance to repeat her exams.

She has seen a bit of the world and advises everybody not to have a break between school and job.

[1]eventually = *schließlich*; [2]self-confidence = *Selbstbewusstsein*

A5 Who said they couldn't do this?

Here are sentences from the conversations Philippa had after she learned about her bad results in the exams. Report what Philippa said.

wbw
60, 33, 59
61, 73

Example:

"I must have some time for myself now."

She said she had to have some time for herself.

1. "I must change my plans."

___

2. "I may do something completely different."

___

3. "I'll find myself a job in Europe."

___

4. "I'll start writing letters right away."

___

5. "I need to find some addresses on the web."

___

6. "Shall I write in English or in German?"

___

7. "I can't speak much German."

___

8. "I won't be able to learn much more before I leave."

___

9. "I don't expect I need to be perfect."

___

10. "I might as well go to the States."

___

A6 Some advice

Read this brochure about opportunities to get to know Europe.

Where to go, who to talk to

Pupils have a variety of opportunities to get to know Europe and to improve their foreign languages. You don't need a lot of money – a lot of projects are funded[1] by the European Union.

School exchanges

Find out what exchanges your school offers with other schools in Europe. Talk to the teachers who are responsible. Perhaps you can join an exchange group.

Ask your foreign language teacher: he or she will usually have some information about longer stays in another European country. They may also know about holiday language courses and where you can find information.

Youth groups

Sports clubs, youth clubs, youth groups of the church or of a political or environmental youth organization – many of them organize international encounters for young people. You could also take part in an international workshop where young people work on one project for a few weeks at a time. If you don't belong to a club or youth group, ask at the local town hall[2] for advice.

Au pair, jobs, work experience

Lots of young people take a break between school and job. They can go abroad as an au pair or they can take an untrained job or take part in an international work experience. Au pair jobs are usually for girls. Be careful, though, as not all organizations are efficient. Talk to your teacher about the various possibilities, search the web or contact international job agencies. If you are in doubt about the quality of an offer, check with a consumer advice[3] centre.

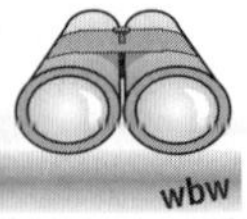

23, 59, 77

a) Find and mark all the imperative forms in the article.

Example: *Find out*

b) Now say what the article advises you to do.

The article It	tells advises	me to …

Example:

The article advises me to talk to the teachers who are responsible.

[1]fund = *bezahlen*; [2]townhall = *Rathaus*; [3]consumer advice centre = *Verbraucherzentrale*

A7 Words available

Find words and phrases from TB A6 which fit these explanations and write the pairs in your exercise book.

1. the participant has to pay for his trip
2. hostels where you can cook your own meals
3. your English should be good
4. about six hours
5. you don't pay anything for your meals and accommodation
6. a light, soft container for fruit
7. a room with a large number of beds
8. you pay 20% less
9. you should look neat and well dressed
10. a job for a part of the year
11. you can't choose where you want to work
12. you don't pay for it

A8 A bit of the world

a) Look at the list of countries in TB A6. Match them with the capitals in the list below and add the language(s) spoken in the country.

capital	country	language(s)
Amsterdam		
Ankara		
Athens		
Berlin		
Berne		
Bratislava		
Brussels		
Budapest		
Copenhagen		
Dublin		
Helsinki		
Lisbon		
London		
Luxembourg		
Madrid		
Oslo		
Paris		
Prague		
Rome		
Sofia		
Stockholm		
Vienna		
Warsaw		

6

b) Choose one country where you'd like to work for some time and write a short text about it. Say why you like this country and what you could do there. Think about the climate / weather, the landscape, the sights the people, etc.

A9 Curriculum Virus

The word processor mixed up this CV. Can you sort it out?
a) Write the correct numbers in the empty boxes and copy the CV as it actually should read.

tip
You'll find help with CVs on pp. 141-142 of your textbook.

Curriculum Vitae

1	Name:	☐	Assadullah Ghauri
2	Address:	☐	Mahmod Ghauri, self-employed businessman Shab Ghauri
3	Date and Place of birth:	☐	programming, cinema, music
4	Parents:	☐	Flößerstr. 25 B
	Schools attended:		
5	primary:	☐	Liebfrauenschule (Sept. 1995 - July 1999)
6	secondary:	☐	English, Technology, Social Science
7	Qualifications:	☐	- good communication skills in German, English and Urdu - practical skills as bilingual telephone attendant - computer skills
8	Favourite subjects:	☐	Carlo-Mierendorff-Schule (Sept. 1999 - present)
9	Work experience:	☐	- part time job in father's textile trading firm - job experience with major Frankfurt computer store (3 weeks)
10	Special skills:	☐	I am at present in year 8 of secondary school (Integrierte Gesamtschule) and will complete secondary school education next year with the certificate "Hauptschulabschluss".
11	Hobbies:	☐	28.09.1988 Frankfurt am Main, Germany
12	Special responsibilities:	☐	deputy systems engineer with CMS-computer club
13	References:	☐	Ms Hanne Burkhardt (form teacher)

________________ Date

________________ Signature

b) Now write out your own CV on a neat sheet of paper.

A10 Curriculum vitae

wbw 82

What will Assadullah Ghauri be doing

- this time next week?
- next summer?
- in five years' time?
- when he is 45?

car - family - hobbies - job - money - place of residence
school - sports - travels - other activites

What will YOU be doing then?

In five years time Assadullah will be driving a ...

This time next week
I won't be working ... because ...

I think I'm sure	I Assadullah ...	will be	travelling ... ...

A11 Perfect future

wbw 82

What will you have done by the time you're 30?
What won't you have done by the time you're 30?

I will have ...

B1 Get connected

a) For each verb in this list, find a "partner noun" from the article in TB B2.

VERB	**NOUN**
call	*caller*
communicate	______
complain	______
inform	______
inquire	______
phone	______
reserve	______
shift	______
summarize	______
switch	______
train	______
work	______

b) Now group your nouns according to their endings.
Try to find more nouns for each category.

-ation	-y	-t
______	______	______
______	______	______
______	______	______
______	______	______

-er	-ing	ø
______	______	______
______	______	______
______	______	______
______	______	______

B2 A call centre agent is something to be

wbw 79, 80, 72, 9, 19

a) Use the verbs from WB B1 to complete these sentences. Use each verb only once. You will have to put them into the correct form before you fill them in.

1. Working in a call centre is very different from sitting at home and ______________ one's friends.
2. A call centre agent must keep cool even if a very unfriendly client ____________________.
3. He or she must be able to ________________ with all kinds of people from all over the world.
4. A call centre agent needs to be well ______________________ about the company's services.
5. Imagine you would like to _________________ a room in a certain hotel and the agent didn't know how to handle the reservation! Wouldn't you ___________________ ?
6. Of course, new agents are _______________ not to panic if someone _______________ about a service they haven't yet heard of.
7. The call centre agents in Dublin usually ____________________ in 8-hour-shifts.
8. When Dublin ________________ off, another Lufthansa call centre in Los Angeles takes over.
9. When the lines in Dublin are overloaded, traffic can be _____________________ to any of the company's other centres anywhere in the world.
10. In order to ___________________ what is important about being a call centre agent, what would you say?

b) Write your answer to no. 10 here:

____

____

____

____

B3 A job interview

CD

a) Listen to this interview between Jane McCrawry and Martina Adler, a German woman.
b) Read the job interview.
c) Listen to the interview again and fill in the questions Jane McCrawry asks.

Jane: Good morning, Ms. Adler. Nice to meet you.

Martina: Good morning.

Jane: Please, take a seat.

Martina: Thank you.

Jane: ____

Martina: Neither, thank you. I had some coffee while I was waiting.

Jane: Right. First of all, I'd like to ask you a few questions about your previous jobs. Err, I understand you came over here directly from Germany?

Martina: Yes, from Dresden. I live in Dresden, in Saxony.

Jane: Ah, lovely. ____

Martina: No, I went there when I set up my travel agency. I was born in Cottbus, but my family moved to Chemnitz when I was a child. So I grew up in Chemnitz, which is not far from Dresden, actually.

Jane: Ah, I see. Err, about your agency - ________________________________

Martina: Well, at first I was quite successful, really. There's lots of tourists in Saxony, you know. But then – I don't know. Everybody seems to use the Internet for bookings these days, or they phone, just like here, you know.

Jane: Yes, certainly.

Martina: And so I got into trouble, financially, I mean. Luckily[1] I gave up before I lost every cent I had put into it.

Jane: Uh-huh. – Ms. Adler, after all this time behind a counter[2], facing your clients directly,

talking to them personally: ____

____

Martina: Well – for a change, really. I know the industry quite well, tourism, I mean. I know how to handle inquiries, impatient[3] customers, international bookings ... And now I'd like to be somewhere else for a while, improve on my English –

Jane: But your English is excellent.

Martina: Oh, thank you.

Jane: Where did you pick[4] it up?

Martina: Pardon me?

Jane: ____

Martina: Oh ... at school. And my mother had friends from England who used to come over and see us in the summer. And I spent some time at Nottingham University when I was a student.

Jane: Very well. Now ... I don't think ... oh yes, about the salary, Ms. Adler, ______________

____

Martina: Well, I don't know. Before I set up my own business I was earning around 1.300, plus bonuses sometimes ...

Jane: Well, I'm afraid it will be different here. As a starting salary, we can only offer 850.

Martina: Uh-huh.

[1]luckily = *glücklicherweise*; [2]counter = *Schalter*; [3]impatient = *ungeduldig;* [4]pick up = *lernen*

Jane: With regular increases, though. And bonuses, and discounts[1] on some Lufthansa services.

Martina: Well, it sounds OK for a start.

Jane: Fine. Now, I don't think I've got any more questions. ______________________________

____

Martina: No, I don't think I've got any questions at the moment. Oh yes, when can you let me know whether I have got the job?

Jane: We hope to make a decision before the weekend. So you can expect to hear from us within the next week. Thank you very much for coming, Ms. Adler.

[1]discount = *Rabatt*

B4 Dos and don'ts at job interviews

wbw 65, 13, 23

Work with a partner. Sort the following into things you should or should not do at a job interview. Use the grid to make sentences like this:

Example: *You should never tell jokes during the interview.*

☺	You should always		
	It's a good idea It will help Sometimes it's OK	to if you	. . .
☹	You should never Definitely don't		

- wear the clothes you find most comfortable
- look interested at all times
- chew gum during the interview
- ~~tell jokes during the interview~~
- shake hands firmly
- switch off your mobile phone before you start the interview
- smile
- wear jeans and sports shoes
- discuss family problems
- smoke during the interview
- be confident
- laugh loudly when the interviewer makes a joke
- make eye contact
- say what your weaknesses[1] are
- discuss the quality of the interview
- answer questions with a simple "yes" or "no"
- plan to arrive about ten minutes early
- say you haven't got any questions about the job
- say "What?" if you haven't understood
- wait until you are offered a chair before you sit down
- discuss family problems

[1]weakness = *Schwäche*

wbw 81, 85, 78, 17, 21

B5 FAQs

In Martina Adler's interview with Jane McCrawry, Martina asks only one question:

"When can you let me know whether I have got the job?"

Here are the endings of seven questions frequently asked by interviewees. Write out the full questions in your exercise book.

... day in this job?

... important duties in this job?

... travelling is normally expected?

... start if you offered me the job?

... are you interviewing for this job?

... overtime or weekend work can I expect?

... previous job holder leave?

B6 dk?

The phrases on the left are from the job offers on pages 92-93 in your textbook. Match them with the phrases on the right to make sure you know what they mean.

1	competitive salaries	☐	no telephone marketing
2	successful candidates	☐	all over the USA
3	across the nation	☐	must speak Spanish very well
4	customer contact area	☐	people who get the job
5	excellent interpersonal, oral, and written communication skills	☐	must be able to talk to and correspond[1] with people properly
6	excellent attendance and punctuality	☐	extra money or advantages you get in addition to your salary
7	excellent data entry and keyboarding skills (55 wpm)	☐	mustn't be off work sick or arrive late
8	must be fluent in Spanish	☐	a hectic, but rather casual[2] office
9	a fun, fast-paced facility	☐	at least average pay, if not more than average
10	an inbound call centre	☐	department where you talk to customers directly
11	employer pays medical, dental, and vision benefits	☐	rewards[3] for people who do a good job
12	absolutely no sales	☐	you will have to answer phone calls
13	casual[2] dress environment	☐	the company will pay your doctor's, dentist's and eye specialist's bills
14	comprehensive benefits package	☐	must be able to type 55 words per minute
15	incentives	☐	you need not wear suits

[1]correspond = *korrespondieren*; [2]casual = *leger, locker*; [3]reward= *Belohnung*

B7 A letter of application

a) Read this job advertisement. Mark words you do not understand. Go back to WB B6 for help and / or use your dictionary, but do not waste time on addresses, abbreviations etc.

Customer Service Representative	
Location: OR - Portland	**Category:** Customer Service
Contact Info	
Company Name: LiveBridge, Inc. **Address:** 7303 SE Lake Road 2nd Floor Portland, OR 97267 **Website:** http://www.livebridge.com	**Contact Name:** Employment Assistant **Phone:** 503 972-6949 **Fax:** **Email:** recruiter-portland@livebridge.com
Job Description	

LiveBridge, a leader in both inbound and outbound customer contact centers, is looking to expand the inbound customer service team near Milwaukie, OR.

ESSENTIAL DUTIES:
Successful candidate will receive phone calls and will perform customer service in the form of problem solving, assisting with completion of applications, receiving catalog orders, or as needed.

THE IDEAL LiveBridge CANDIDATE:
- Ability to assist the client through clear and professional verbal communications
- Solid computer familiarity with data entry skills at $\geq$ 25 WPM
- Highly motivated with above average customer service and sales skills
- Flexibility for various morning, swing or night shifts including the commitment of Saturday &/or Sunday shift
- Demonstrates strong work ethic and positive team player attitude

WHAT LiveBridge OFFERS IN RETURN:
- Customer service training
- Guaranteed $7/HR weekly paid wage + performance driven bonuses
- Positive, business casual work environment
- Skill development and opportunities to advance within our growing company

Due to continuous growth, we are looking to add to our team immediately. If you are interested in learning, growing and succeeding in a fast-paced environment, we'd like to visit with you. Interviews conducted Monday – Friday, 9AM – 4PM. Please apply by email only.

b) Now have a look at the phrases below. Check any words you do not understand in the dictionary or consult pp. 143-144 in your textbook.

- I enclose a copy of
- I have had over two years experience
- I trained as a
- available for an interview
- my skills and experience
- I am used to
- I look forward
- working irregular hours
- I am writing to apply for
- using my own initiative
- working freelance
- act as referees
- looking for a new challenge
- a suitable applicant for this job

c) Now use the phrases to complete this letter of application:

Back Forward Reload **Home** **Search**

Location: recruiter-portland@livebridge.com What's Related

Gentlemen:

SUBJECT: vacancy for a customer sales representative

__________ the position of Customer Service Representative advertised[1] on your website. __________ my resumé and the names and addresses of two people who are prepared to __________.

As you will see from my resumé, __________ working as a part time agent in an inbound call center while I finished high school, so __________ performing[2] various kinds of customer service. When I left school __________ keyboard operator in a small typesetting company[3], which closed down as the typesetting[4] is nowadays done by the publishers[5] themselves. After __________ for some time I am now __________ in a professional environment.

I enjoy using my own initiative and am used to __________. In addition to this, I think __________ make me __________. I am __________ at any time.

Thank you for considering[6] my application. __________ to hearing from you.

Sincerely yours

I. McApple

[1]advertise = *ausschreiben;* [2]perform = *verrichten, erfüllen;* [3]typesetting company = *Schriftsetzerei;* [4]typesetting = *Schriftsatz;* [5]publisher = *Verlag;* [6]consider = *in Betracht ziehen*

B8 What are they going to do?

Read TB B6 on page 93 again.

wbw 20, 85

a) What is Sylvie going to do on the day of her interview? Complete these sentences using the "going to-future".

1. ______________________________ early.

2. ______________________________ her light blue suit.

3. She is not ______________________________ much for breakfast.

4. As she does not know when the buses go, she ______________________________.

5. After the interview ______________________________ at the office.

b) What about Mr Müllerleile's day? Ask questions using the "going to-future".

1. ______________________________ train to the office?

2. ______________________________ the applicants in small groups?

3. ______________ Jane ______________________________?

4. ______________________________ Elaine for lunch?

Welcome to Scotland

7

A1 Writing letters

a) This is a letter to the Scottish Tourist Board. What's wrong with it? Find the mistakes. Decide what other changes you would make.

> *tip* Look at page 144-146 in your textbook for help in writing a formal letter.

```
                                                        Alf Johnson
                                                        Ralph Ormond
                                                        75 Queens Rd
                                                        London W11 DH5
Scottish Tourist Board
PO Box 705
Edinburgh
Scotland EH4 3EU

         Dear Mr or Mrs Whatsyername?,

Our english teacher, Mr Sumner, came into our class the other day, I
think it was on tuesday after the break, and said we were going to do a
project on scotland. So me and my friend Ralph thought we would try and
get good marks¹ for a change, which is why we're writing this letter.
It's not that we don't like english, it's just that Mr Sumner is always
going on for hours about things that are sooo boring. You've no idea how
difficult it is to keep awake.
Anyway, it would be absolutely brill if you could send us stacks² of
brochures and pictures about scotland. Don't leave it too long either!
We need the stuff at the beginning of next week.

Love and kisses
Alf and Ralph
```

[1]mark = *Note*; [2]stacks = *jede Menge*

b) Write the letter in the correct form in your exercise book.

A2 Scottish facts

Read "Scotland" (TB A2) again. Then match the words and expressions.

the Highlands	tree trunk
the Lowlands	discovered in the 1970s
a lot of sheep farming	national drink
the last Scottish prince	the Southern Uplands
North Sea oil and gas	football clubs
the Scottish flag	oats, milk, water, salt
Edinburgh	mountains, lochs, moors
Celtic Glasgow and Glasgow Rangers	stuffed sheep's stomach
caber	defeated in 1746
porridge	capital
haggis	the best farming area
whisky	Saint Andrew's Cross

A3 Scottish dreams

wbw 12, 22, 84

Complete the sentences. Use your imagination!

1. If I were in Scotland, I would ____________________.
2. If I travelled to Edinburgh, I would not ____________________.
3. If I could choose something Scottish to eat, I ____________________.
4. If I went to the Highland Games, I ____________________.
5. If I were a Celtic Glasgow fan, ____________________.
6. If I could spend my holidays in Scotland, ____________________.
7. If I had a Scottish penfriend, ____________________.
8. If I saw Nessie, ____________________.
9. If someone gave me a kilt, ____________________.
10. If I met the Queen's husband, ____________________.
11. If I ____________________.
12. ____________________.

A4 A kind of humour

*Heaven is where the police are English,
the cooks are French,
the mechanics are German,
the lovers are Italian and
it is all organized by the Swiss.*

**Hell is where the police are German,
the cooks are English,
the mechanics are French,
the lovers are Swiss and
it is all organized by the Italians.**

Do you agree? Think of more prejudices. Work in pairs and present your ideas to the class.

A5 Prejudiced comparisons?

a) Compare nationalities.
Example:
People think that English policemen behave[1] more politely than German policemen.
People think that German policemen behave less politely than English policemen.
People think that (work efficiently)

wbw 10, 31

(cook deliciously)

(organize successfully)

[1] *behave* = sich benehmen

b) Write down more national prejudices and compare. Use the phrases in the box.

wbw 31, 4

speak loudly • dance / dress elegantly • behave friendly • learn successfully • be open-minded • be punctual

People think that

c) Discuss your ideas in class.

A6 How can you do it?

wbw 31

In WB A5 you had to think about national prejudices using adverbs and adjectives in comparisons. Now use adverbs to describe everyday actions. Start by adding adverbs to these word roses.
You could also prepare classroom posters that help you to write interesting texts.

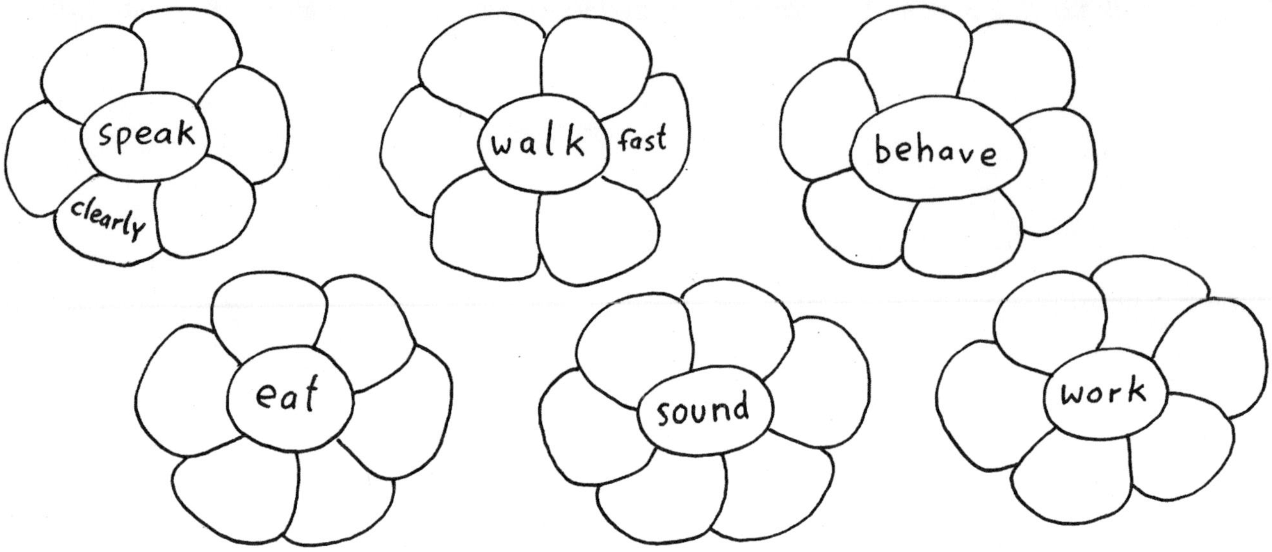

A7 Success at the Highland Games

wbw 10

Look at the results from these Highland Games and compare.
Use *higher / highest / further / furthest / better / best / worse / worst.*

Sportsman	Throwing the weight	Throwing the hammer	Playing the pipes
John McEnroy	13 feet	118 feet	9 points
Andrew McCarthy	13 feet 6 inches	122 feet	5 points
Jack Fitzgerald	12 feet 6 inches	110 feet	12 points
Sean O'Neill	13 feet	120 feet	8 points
Dick McWilliam	11 feet 6 inches	121 feet	6 points

Examples:

John McEnroy threw the weight higher than Jack Fitzgerald.

Andrew McCarthy threw the hammer furthest of all.

Andrew McCarthy played the pipes worse than John McEnroy.

wbw 37, 8, 16

A8 Scottish inventions

Who invented what? Read A6 in your textbook and find out. Write sentences using the passive.

car tyres
raincoat
adhesive stamps
bicycle
lane surface
US Navy
telephone
television

Alexander Graham Bell
John Boyd Dunlop
Kirkpatrick MacMillan
John MacAdam
John Logie Baird
John Chalmers
Charles MacIntosh
John Paul Jones

Car tyres were invented by ______________________

____

____

____

____

____

____

A9 Edinburgh

a) Look at the following texts on Edinburgh.

Text 1

Edinburgh is the capital city of Scotland. It is also the country's cultural, political and commercial centre. It is situated near the east coast between the Firth of Forth and the Pentland Hills. The city is built on seven hills. The Old Town is overlooked by the castle, which dates from the 11th century. The area between the castle and the Palace of Holyroodhouse is the official residence of the Queen in Edinburgh. It is known as "The Royal Mile". The New Town was built between 1767 and 1800 as a suburb[1] of the city. Princes Street is its main road. There are many fashionable shops and modern hotels. Factories in Edinburgh produce chemicals and pharmaceutics, electronic equipment, engineering products, textiles, beer and graphics. Modern rail and road communications link Edinburgh with the rest of Great Britain. There is an airport ten kilometres outside the city.

Text 2

Scotland is famous for giving its guests a warm welcome. Nowhere is this more true than in Edinburgh! Edinburgh has all the advantages of a capital city together with a friendly atmosphere. It is a city of contrasts. There is the Old Town overlooked by the castle, with over nine hundred years of history. And there is the Palace of Holyroodhouse, home to the tragic Mary Stuart, standing alongside the grand architecture of the New Town. Steep[2], winding[3] streets look down over rooftops and up to high spires[4] and the castle battlements[5]. Scotland's capital seems more like Athens than a typical British city. You will find excellent shopping facilities, a wide variety of restaurants, theatres, art galleries and concert halls. You can enjoy a fantastic tradition of music and drama festivals. You will never forget this civilised, beautiful and fascinating city.

b) Compare the texts:

1. Underline the facts in each of the texts in red.
2. Put a circle around the adjectives in both texts in green. Look up any adjectives you do not understand in your dictionary.
3. What information is included in both texts? What information is given only in text 1? Or only in text 2? Can you think why?
4. Where do you think you might find each of the texts? Who do you think each is written for?
5. Compare your work with that of your partner. Discuss your answers in class.

[1]suburb = *Vorort*; [2]steep = *steil*; [3]winding = *gewunden*; [4]spire = *Turmspitze*; [5]battlements = *Zinnen*

A10 Emigration

We're the emigrant ones, not the last in the line.
We're leaving, leaving, leaving, till there's nowhere left to go.

a) What comes to your mind when you think of *emigration*. Make a word rose.

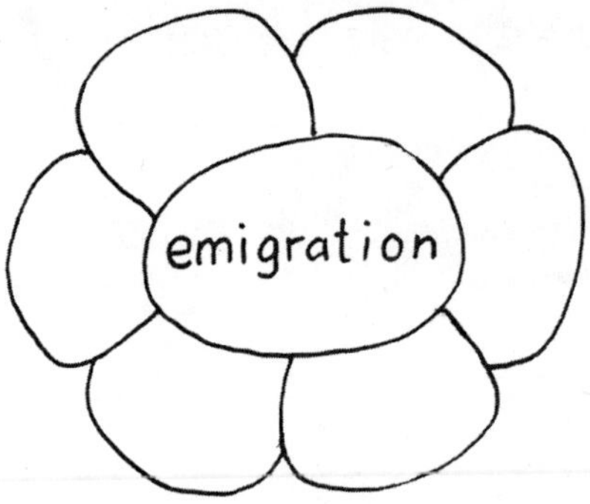

b) Categorize your findings and add more ideas: reasons – problems in their new homes – ...
c) Why would you / did you emigrate from your home country? Make notes and write a text.
d) Make an acrostic:

E ______________________________
M ______________________________
I ______________________________
G ______________________________
R ______________________________
A ______________________________
T ______________________________
I ______________________________
O ______________________________
N ______________________________

B1 Royal arithmetic

Read TB B1 and B3 and answer the following questions. Remember that Mary was born at the end of 1542.

1. How many husbands did Mary Stuart have? ____________
2. What year was Mary sent to France? ____________
3. How old was Mary when she became Queen of France? ____________
4. How old was her husband when he became King of France? ____________
5. How old was Mary when her mother died? ____________
6. What year did Mary's first husband die? ____________
7. How old was Mary when her son was born? ____________
8. How old was she when she went to England? ____________
9. At what age was Mary beheaded? ____________

Your figures should add up to 3252. ____________

B2 The ifs of Mary's life

wbw 12, 84, 22

1. If Mary's father had not died so early, she would not have become Queen of Scots at the age of six days.
2. If Mary's mother had not been French, they ________ ________ ________ travelled to France.
3. If Mary's mother had been Protestant, she ____________ ____________ stayed in Scotland.
4. If Mary's first husband had not died, she ________ not ________ ____________ Lord Darnley.
5. If Darnley had not been unfaithful, Mary ________ not ____________ chosen other advisers.
6. If Rizzio had not come to Scotland, the Scottish nobles ______________________________ ______________________________.
7. If Lord Darnley had not been killed, Mary ______________________________ ______________________________ Bothwell.
8. If Mary had gone to Scandinavia with Bothwell, ______________________________ ________ ______________________________.
9. ______________________________ ______________________________.

B3 Mary's life

wbw 65, 80

What went wrong in Mary's life? Two of her servants are talking about her after the execution. They of course know what she should have done better. Use the parts on the left and combine them with the information on the right to make sentences.

She should have		
She shouldn't have	*plotted against Elizabeth*	*stayed in Scotland*
	kept her son	*become Protestant*
She ought to have	*married Edward*	*remained Queen*
She ought not to have	*brought Rizzio with her*	*been alive today*
	been executed	*married Darnley*
She might have	*gone to France*	
She might not have		

She ought to have married Edward. Then she might have been alive today.

____

____

____

____

____

____

B4 A biography

Write the biography of someone (still alive) who you admire[1] in your exercise book. It might be a friend, a relative or someone you have never met. Here are some phrases to help you:

... was born in ... on ... . His / Her father / mother / parents was / were ... . When he / she was ... years old ... . At the age of ... he / she learned ... . After school ... . When he / she was ... . Today he / she lives ... . I admire / like him / her because ... .

[1]admire = *bewundern*

B5 The same or not the same

Use a dictionary to help you find synonyms and / or opposites for the following words:

	synonym	opposite
1. handsome		
2. defeat		
3. execute		
4. mysterious		
5. faithful		
6. pregnant		
7. uprising		
8. struggles		
9. bitter		
10. jealous		

B6 This is your life

This is your life is a successful TV show. Famous people are confronted with events and persons from their lives. The compère[1] greets them like this: "John Smith. This is your life." Then they meet friends and relatives in the studio. At first only the voices of the friends and relatives are heard. They hide behind a screen and the famous person has to guess who they are.
In groups of four or five prepare such a TV show about Mary Queen of Scots. Bring her and her relatives back to life. You will need a compère, Mary, and some of the following people:

her mother – childhood friends – the Dauphin – John Knox – Rizzio – Darnley – Bothwell – her son James – ...

What will the guests say behind the screen? Will Mary greet them? She will probably not always be happy to see them!

[1]compère = *Conférencier*

wbw 85

B7 Guess who!

Twenty questions

Split up into groups of three or four. Two groups work together.
Group 1 must think of a famous person.
Group 2 must guess who this person is by asking questions which can only be answered with "yes" or "no".
If group 2 does not guess the person after 20 questions then group 1 wins the game.
Now it's group 2's turn to think up a famous person.

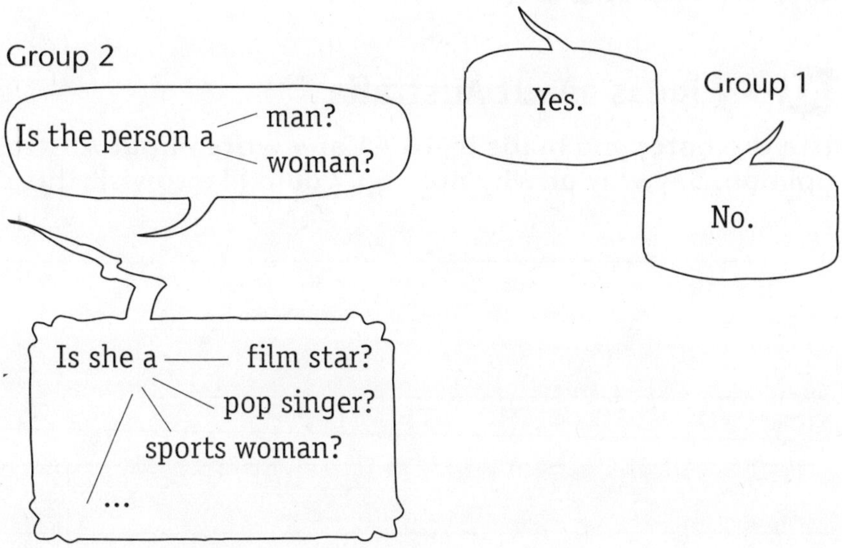

B8 The UK Quiz

How many of these questions can you answer? Try to find the answers to the others in an encyclopaedia or on the Internet.

1. What is the capital city of Wales?
   a) Swansea b) Cardiff c) Edinburgh

2. Where is the highest mountain in the United Kingdom?
   a) in Scotland b) in Wales c) in Northern Ireland
3. What is the biggest city in Britain?
   a) Birmingham b) Manchester c) London

4. How many countries make up Great Britain?
   a) three b) four c) five
5. What is the Union Jack?
   a) a British ship b) the British flag c) the border between Scotland and England
6. In which country can you find road signs in two languages?
   a) Scotland b) England c) Wales

7. What is the largest city in Scotland?
   a) Aberdeen b) Glasgow c) Edinburgh
8. What colours are in the English flag?
   a) blue & white b) red & white c) red, white & blue
9. Which of these countries does not have its own bank notes?
   a) Northern Ireland b) Scotland c) Wales
10. Which country is in the United Kingdom but not in Great Britain?
    a) Scotland b) Northern Ireland c) Wales

11. What is the capital city of Northern Ireland?
    a) Cardiff b) Belfast c) Dublin

8 Down under

A1 My ideas about Australia

Use the notes you made in TB A1 and write about Australia. Include facts and your opinion. Say why or why not you would like to visit this country.

____

____

____

____

____

A2 What is a kangaroo?

a) Complete the text. Then compare it to the original in your textbook.

Do you know w ________ a kangaroo i ________ called a k ________ ?

Well, about 200 y ________ ago, a w ________ man w ________ travelling

th ________ Australia and he m ________ an Aborigine in the b ________ .

The A ________ had n ________ heard a white m ________ speak be ________

and of course he d ________ not speak En ________ .

The white man s ________ a strange a ________ hopping p ________ .

"What i ________ that?" he cr ________ .

The Aborigine lo ________ at him, and the hopping an ________ .

"K ________ ?" he as ________ in his na ________ Aboriginal

la ________, which means "What d ________ you s ________ ?".

The Englishman thanked h ________ and wr ________ down the

n ________ of the animal. in his little bo ________ . Even today, people are using

the wrong name. But at least one word from an Aboriginal language hops on.

b) Read your completed text and find examples for these tenses. Write them down in your exercise book.

simple present	simple past	past perfect simple
present progressive	past progressive	simple

c) Explain the use of these tenses to a partner.

A3 Gemma

Write down the most important facts about Gemma. Start like this:

Gemma is Australian. She lives on a cattle station in __________

____

____

____

____

A4 Places

a) Find the words for these definitions in Gemma's story:

1. a place where cows are bred[1]: __________
2. a school where pupils live and work: __________
3. a place where you can buy a drink: __________
4. a place where you wait for the bus: __________
5. a house which has only one storey[2]: __________
6. a place outside the house where you can sit under a roof: __________

b) Write definitions for these words:

1. a hut: __________
2. the butcher's: __________
3. the station: __________
4. a swimming pool: __________
5. the coast: __________
6. the outback: __________

[1]breed = *züchten*; [2]storey = *Etage*

A5 A letter to Gemma

Write a letter to Gemma.

1. Comment on what she wrote: I didn't know … It was interesting to read about …
2. Tell her about YOUR life, your school, your spare time, your plans, …
3. Ask her questions.

Example: *How often did you see your parents?*
What do you do during the weekend on your cattle station?

A6 More about Kate

Read this information about Kate and write about her.

Born: 27 November 1982
Family: mother Margaret, father Richard, and sister Ruth, 15
Favourite food: Mexican
Favourite film: The Green Mile
Favourite band: Savage Garden
Hobbies: running, travelling
Plans for the future: to study medicine and become a doctor
What she hates: rain and snow
Dream: to travel into space

A7 A loner

What do you think about Kate's long walk through the bush?
a) Make notes about her walk.
Copy this table first, then fill it with your thoughts.

Kate	interesting	dangerous	scary	not my thing
18				

b) Use your notes to speak about Kate's adventure.

A8 In her own words

Report what Kate said. Use the quotes and the words in the box.

wbw 60, 59, 61, 73

mention, report, explain, admit, think

"In the first two weeks I only met about four people."
"I came across an emu with chicks."
"Males look after the chicks."
"It saw me coming and it didn't like me."
"It walked right up to my face."
"I was scared. It was a lot bigger than me."
"It wanted to scare me away."
"I stopped and stared at it. It stared at me."
"In the end, the emu turned round and ran back down the path."
"After some weeks I was getting closer to the coast."
"I took off my shoes and walked without them."
"The sun came out and my feet got terribly sunburnt."
"I thought, I can't have a wheelchair, so I have to walk."
"I was walking in pain."

Example: *Kate admitted that she had been scared.*

A9 Let's talk Strine

Do you understand this sentence?
"So this arvo when you sit down with your mates for a barbie and to watch the footy, try telling them some true blue jokes."

CD

a) Listen to the CD and try to speak Australian.

Australian word	Meaning
arvo	afternoon
Aussie	Australian
barbie	barbecue
beaut	beautiful
bush	the countryside
chook	chicken
dunny	toilet
fair dinkum	true, honest
fairy floss	candy floss
footy	Australian football
g'day	hello
good on ya	good for you
Hooroo	goodbye
how's it goin'?	how are you?
mate	friend
outback	interior[1] of Australia
Oz	Australia
true blue	genuinely Australian
tucker	food
woop woop	small town
yakka	work
station	farm

b) Can you speak Australian English? Work with a partner and try to use some of the words in short dialogues. What would this be in Strine?
Example:
A. Hello.
B. Hello, how are you?
A. Fine. Do you want to come to a barbecue this afternoon?
B. Sure. What's for food?
A. Australian chicken. And later we can have a football match.
B. Good for you.
A. Right. Good bye.
B. Good bye.

c) Listen to the dialogue on the CD and practise it with your partner. You can also make your own dialogues.

[1]interior = *Innere*

A10 National geography

Find this information about your home country and about Australia.

	home country:	Australia
size in sq.km:		
population:		
capital:		
other big cities:		
climate / weather:		
rivers, mountains, …		
other important information:		

B1 A sad story

Read B1 in your textbook once more.
Write down what you think is the most shocking sentence in the report.

Can you say why?

I think it's shocking to

because

Now listen to your classmates' sentences and to their reasons.

B2 An Aboriginal family

Fill in the family tree and some dates.

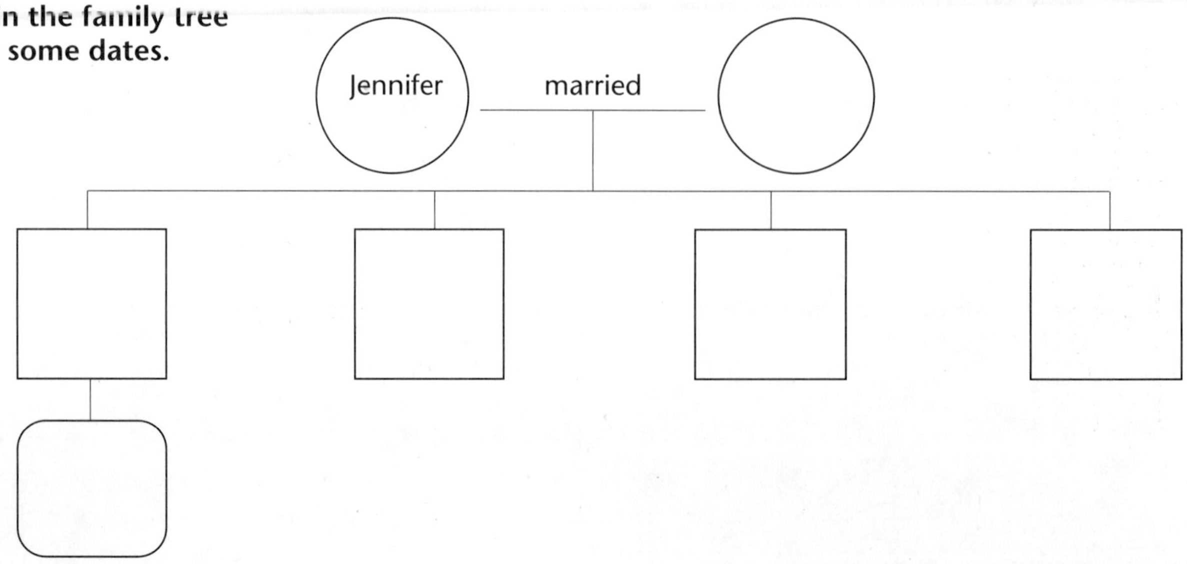

B3 Grace's life

Fill in the years.

Grace was born in ___________ .

She was sent to Cootamundra children's home in __________ , when she was only

_______ years old.

In __________ , when she was __________ years old, she had to work as a children's nurse.

Her daughter Fiona was born in __________ . When she was _________ years old she had to

leave her family and live in Cootamundra. This happened in the year ________ .

___________ years later, in ________ she returned to her family.

B4 The girls

a) Find out what happened to each of the girls. Use the passive.

wbw 37, 16, 8

		as a children's nurse
	(send out)	to get a job
Jennifer	(bear)	as a cook
Grace	(take)	around 1890
Esther	(train)	to the babies' home in Rockdale
May	(send)	to leave her family at the age of 11
Fiona	(teach)	to Cootamundra Home
	(force)	by coach to Cootamundra
		reading, writing and arithmetic

b) Change these active sentences into the passive voice:

During the summer, we need extra help.

Kangaroo hunters kill a whole load of kangaroos.

They make pet food out of them.

Not many people eat kangaroo meat.

The dingos will attack the cattle.

Then the doggers will kill the dingos.

When someone has an accident they call the "Flying doctor".

Someone takes the person back to one of the towns.

Male emus look after the chicks.

Emus can kick and hurt people badly.

People have caught lots of emus in the past few years.

They put the emus on a barbie and grill them.

wbw 33, 66

B5 And you?

What did you do then?

When I was eleven years old, I ______________________________

I could ______________________________

I was allowed to ______________________________

I was able to ______________________________

When I was fourteen years old, I ______________________________

I got ______________________________

I had ______________________________

I went to ______________________________

I spent my holidays in ______________________________

I ______________________________

B6 Verb detective

wbw 67, 66

Find the missing forms for these verbs. They all come from A2 and B1.

simple present	simple past	past participle	German
write			
hear			
meet			
speak			
see			
cry			
hop			
am/is/are			
come			
think			
take			
give			
die			
send			
teach			

B7 An Aboriginal life

a) Which of these sentences are true (t), false (f) or not in the text (n) in B3 in your textbooks ?

1. Sally came home from school and was crying. ☐
2. Nan was upset because the children didn't like her. ☐
3. Sally had not realised before that her grandmother was black. ☐
4. Jill and Sally shared a room. ☐
5. Jill doesn't mind being an Aborigine. ☐
6. The white Australians at the school didn't like Aborigines. ☐
7. Sally doesn't know very much about Aborigines. ☐
8. Sally likes animals. ☐

b) Correct the false sentences.

B8 In other words

Find words or expressions in the text which mean more or less the same:

a. I stood without moving: ______________________

b. I was very much astonished: ______________________

c. stupid: ______________________

d. you think I am easily tricked: ______________________

e. I found the courage: ______________________

f. Many students at the school disapprove[1] of Aboriginals: ______________________

g. unable to think clearly: ______________________

[1]disapprove of s.o. = *etwas gegen jn. haben*

B9 What they said

wbw 60, 59, 61, 73

Report the following statements and questions.

a. Sally: "Nan, what's wrong?"

Sally asked Nan ____

b. Sally to Nan: "What are you crying for?"

____

c. Nan: "You bloody kids don't want me, you want a bloody white grandmother, I'm black."

____

____

d. Sally to Jill: "Did you know Nan was black?"

___

e. Jill to Sally: "You're really dumb, sometimes."

___

f. Jill to Sally: "Look at Nan. Does she look Indian?"

___

g. Sally to Jill: "I've never really thought about how she looks. Maybe she comes from some Indian tribe we don't know about."

___

___

h. Sally to Jill: "What's a boong?"

___

i. Jill to Sally: "I can't believe you've never heard the word 'boong'".

___

j. Jill to Sally: "Haven't you ever listened to the kids in school?"

___

B10 Really dumb, sometimes

wbw 3, 4, 31

Find all the adjectives and adverbs in TB B3 and put them in two lists according to their usage in the text.

adjectives

wrong

___ ___

___ ___

___ ___

___ ___

___ ___

___ ___

___ ___

adverbs

early

___

___

___

___

___

___

___

B11 A last look

Write about Australia. Choose between
- **an acrostic,**
- **a two word poem or**
- **a diamond poem.**

Here's an example of a diamond poem. Find its structure before your start.

past
sad, dark
suffering, stealing, killing
hope, integration, brotherhood, harmony
changing, understanding, learning,
eager[1], together
future

line 1: a noun ____________________

line 2: ____________________

line 3: ____________________

line 4: ____________________

line 5: ____________________

line 6: ____________________

line 7: the opposite of the first noun

[1]eager = *eifrig*

B12 A different sport

Read this text about the boomerang.
The kind of boomerang used in sports comes back to the thrower. It has a curved[1] surface[2] on one side and a flat surface on the other. As the boomerang flies, the air flows across the two sides differently. As it flies, the boomerang spins[3]. The spinning boomerang comes full circle back to its starting point.

Now look at these pictures. They show how the boomerang works.
Write one sentence from the text under each picture. Do not use a dictionary.

[1]curved = *gewölbt;* [2]surface = *Fläche;* [3]spin = *herumwirbeln*

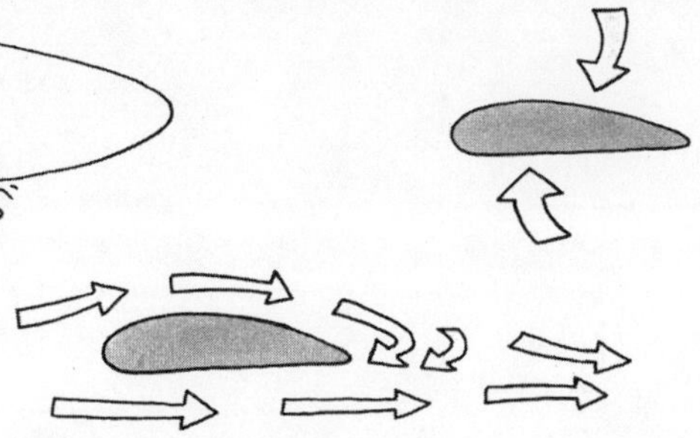

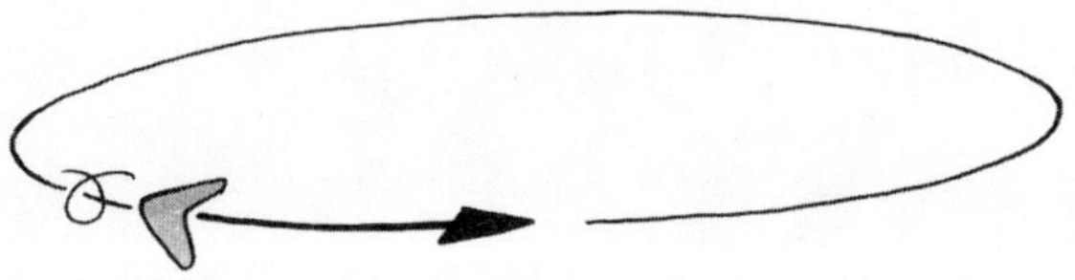

portfolio

Portfolio

Was ich jetzt nach fünf Jahren Englisch kann:

Ich kann über diese Dinge sprechen und schreiben:

____

____

____

____

Mein Lieblingsthema in diesem Jahr war: ______________________________

Mein Lieblingstext in diesem Jahr war: ______________________________

Ich habe außerhalb der Schule Englisch gesprochen: ______________________________

____

____

Ich habe diese Dinge im Englischunterricht hergestellt: ______________________________

____

____

____

Meine Englischarbeiten / Tests in diesem Jahr waren

○ **sehr gut** ○ **gut** ○ **OK** ○ **nicht so gut**

Sie waren

○ **besser als letztes Jahr** ○ **so wie letztes Jahr** ○ **schlechter als letztes Jahr**

Für das nächste Jahr nehme ich mir vor:

____

____

____

Zum

ENGLISCHLERNEN

ist/sind für mich wichtig:

	Ja	Nein		Ja	Nein
Vokabeln	◯	◯	Lernspiele	◯	◯
Texte lesen	◯	◯	Dialoge	◯	◯
Geschichten schreiben	◯	◯	Tests	◯	◯
Geschichten hören	◯	◯	Lieder	◯	◯
Auswendiglernen	◯	◯	Aussprache	◯	◯
Computerübungen	◯	◯	Diskussionen	◯	◯
Grammatik	◯	◯	Hören	◯	◯
Landeskunde	◯	◯	Schreiben	◯	◯
Projekte	◯	◯	Übersetzen	◯	◯
Videos	◯	◯	___________	◯	◯

Was ich jetzt kann:

SCHREIBEN

	Kein Problem.	Ich mache ein paar Fehler.	Das muss ich noch üben.
Ich kann mir zu einem Thema Notizen machen.	◯	◯	◯
Ich kann kurze Texte über mich schreiben.	◯	◯	◯
Ich kann einfache Gedichte schreiben.	◯	◯	◯
Ich kann mit einfachen Sätzen über ein Ereignis berichten.	◯	◯	◯
Ich kann kurze persönliche Briefe schreiben.	◯	◯	◯
Ich kann die Ergebnisse eines Projekts schriftlich darstellen.	◯	◯	◯
Ich kann das Wichtigste aus einem Text schriftlich zusammenfassen.	◯	◯	◯
Ich kann eine Geschichte schreiben.	◯	◯	◯

portfolio

Was ich jetzt kann:

SPRECHEN

	Kein Problem.	Ich mache ein paar Fehler.	Das muss ich noch üben.
Ich kann etwas mithilfe von Notizen sagen.	○	○	○
Ich kann mich zu Bildern äußern.	○	○	○
Ich kann den Inhalt einer Geschichte oder eines Films kurz wiedergeben.	○	○	○
Ich kann anderen über eigene Erlebnisse berichten.	○	○	○
Ich kann über meine Träume, Hoffnungen und Ängste erzählen.	○	○	○
Ich kann meine Meinung zu einem Problem äußern.	○	○	○
Ich kann eine Interview durchführen.	○	○	○
Ich kann erklären, wie etwas funktioniert.	○	○	○

Wie ich lerne:

VOKABELN

	Kein Problem.	Ich mache ein paar Fehler.	Das muss ich noch üben.
Ich kann Wörter im Vokabelanhang des TB nachschlagen.	○	○	○
Ich kann ein Wörterbuch benutzen.	○	○	○
Ich kann unbekannte Wörter in einem Text erraten.	○	○	○
Ich kann mir Ersatzwörter ausdenken, wenn mir ein Wort nicht gleich einfällt.	○	○	○
Ich kann mir neue Wörter gut merken.	○	○	○

Ich lerne neue Wörter am besten

- ○ aus dem Buch.
- ○ wenn ich sie der Reihe nach aufschreibe.
- ○ wenn ich sie auf Kärtchen schreibe.
- ○ mit Wortfeldern und Wortnetzen.
- ○ wenn mich jemand abfragt.
- ○ wenn ich sie in Texten benutze.
- ○ ____________________

Was ich jetzt kann:

LESEN

	Kein Problem.	Ich mache ein paar Fehler.	Das muss ich noch üben.
Ich kann die Anweisungen im TB und WB verstehen.	○	○	○
Ich kann von längeren Texten so viel verstehen, dass ich weiß, worum es geht.	○	○	○
Ich kann unbekannte Wörter in Texten erraten.	○	○	○
Ich kann in Texten wichtige Stellen finden und markieren.	○	○	○
Ich kann einen Text gliedern / in Abschnitte einteilen.	○	○	○
Ich kann in Texten erkennen, wo es um Gefühle und wo es um Sachinformationen geht.	○	○	○
Ich kann E-Mails und Internet-Texte verstehen.	○	○	○
Ich kann Anzeigen, Broschüren und Speisekarten usw. verstehen.	○	○	○
Ich habe bereits längere Texte gelesen, die nicht in meinem Textbook oder Workbook waren.	○	○	○

Was ich jetzt kann:

HÖREN

	Kein Problem.	Ich mache ein paar Fehler.	Das muss ich noch üben.
Ich kann von Hörtexten so viel verstehen, dass ich weiß, worum es geht.	○	○	○
Ich kann von Liedern und Gedichten das Wichtigste verstehen.	○	○	○
Ich kann jemanden verstehen, der amerikanisches Englisch spricht.	○	○	○
Ich kann mir zu Hörtexten Notizen machen.	○	○	○
Ich kann auch Texte mit Hintergrundgeräuschen verstehen.	○	○	○
Ich kann die Anweisungen meiner Lehrerin / meines Lehrers verstehen.	○	○	○

portfolio

Wie ich lerne: **SPRECHEN**

Englisch zu sprechen fällt mir leicht, wenn

- ◯ ich erst einen Moment Zeit zum Nachdenken habe.
- ◯ ich mir zur Sicherheit ein paar Notizen machen kann.
- ◯ mich das Thema interessiert.
- ◯ ich mich an einer Diskussion beteilige.
- ◯ ich nicht bei jedem Fehler gleich unterbrochen werde.
- ◯ ich außerhalb der Schule mit jemandem rede.
- ◯ ______________________________

Bildquellen:

S. 3 Thomas Haffner, Berlin
S. 10 IFA Bilderteam / BCI, Frankfurt
S. 11 li.: IFA Bilderteam / Ventura, Frankfurt
re.: IFA Bilderteam / Aberham, Frankfurt
S. 24 dpa, Udo Bernhart, Frankfurt
S. 54 MEV / Susanne Holzmann
S. 56 o.li.: IFA Bilderteam / Aberham, Frankfurt
o.re.: Mauritius / Nägele, Mittenwald
mi.li.: Mauritius / World Pictures, Mittenwald
mi.re.: IFA Bilderteam / E. Pott, Frankfurt
u.re.: IFA Bilderteam / W. Lauer, Frankfurt

Lösung zu WB 1A1

3. between 13 and 20
7. about 1, 500, 000